WHY WE DO WHAT WE DO:

Christian Worship in the African-American Tradition

by

Joseph Jones, D.Min.

1

WHY WE DO WHAT WE DO: CHRISTIAN WORSHIP IN THE AFRICAN-AMERICAN TRADITION

Copyright © 2006 by R.H. Boyd Publishing Corporation

6717 Centennial Blvd.
Nashville, Tennessee 37209-1049

ISBN 1-58942309-7

Printed in the United States of America.

DEDICATION

❧

This book is dedicated to my wife of 37 years, Dr. Althea Taylor-Jones, who was inexhaustibly supportive and sustaining, and to the members of the Zion Memorial Baptist Church, who were very patient during this endeavor.

TABLE OF CONTENTS

Chapter 6

ACKNOWLEDGMENTS

I would like to acknowledge several individuals whose assistance was instrumental in enabling me to write this book.

For the contents of this book, I am deeply indebted to those whose contributions to my own world view and life have been important. Two of those people are my mother, Rebie Maggie Moss, and my stepfather, Kit Clifton Moss, who took me to church at an early age, where I was able to receive a spiritual foundation and strength to survive in a world of oppression and remain reasonably sane.

I'm much obliged to the members of Zion Memorial Baptist Church. This group of supportive parishioners was very patient during the endeavor to complete this book.

The most significant support and encouragement of all has come from my wife of 37 years, Althea Taylor-Jones, whom I wooed and won in the bright days of our youth at Tennessee State University. She has been inexhaustibly supportive and sustaining for the entire time.

Above all, I owe God everything. To God be all glory and honor forever and ever.

Introduction and Overview

My interest in writing this book about African-American worship emanates from my experience as an African-American Baptist preacher in the southern United States. The African-American Baptist Church is an American Black cultured denomination within the mainstream of the United States in that it has evolved out of the Baptist tradition of Protestantism.

The following information on African-American worship is not intended to imply that all African-American congregations look and sound the same on Sunday morning at worship time, but is an effort to highlight some of its characteristics. The purpose of this book is to emphasize the worship tradition of African Americans as distinctive, as special, not better or worse than other types of worship, but to understand it as having a distinct history, tradition, and practice.

There are different styles of worship in the African-American church, which vary from church to church. Some determinant factors are responsible for these variations. In her book, *African American Christian Worship*, Melva Wilson Costen makes the following statement:

> Although African Americans share many common worship practices, one should not assume that all African American congregations will or should exhibit homogeneous styles of worship. Different situations and circumstances under which exposure to Christianity took place for each congregation, denomination (history and theological orientation), geography, and social life-styles are significant determinants of worship.[1]

Though there is a difference in the style of worship, there are also distinctive, discernable patterns. One historian pointed out: "The fact that Black people have uniqueness of expression in worship from the larger society is today beyond dispute. This uniqueness stems from the influence of Africa on African Americans and the influence of being persons who have lived in Western culture on the margins."[2]

African-American people, after being forced to live in a strange land, were enslaved and treated as less than human. Equality was not an item on the agenda for African Americans. White oppression and institutional racism were the order of the day. African natives were brought to this strange land but not allowed to be participants. The whole process was an attempt to erase the past from their minds, which is a common historical experience. Because of this common history, there is a uniqueness in the way African Americans express themselves in worship.

Each of us is born within a certain tradition, which has a great influence in shaping our lives. Information is handed down from generation to generation. The basis of socialization, whether from the world of nature or the family environment, is a major influence on the way we conduct our lives. This holds true with African-American worship. Traditional beliefs and certain discernable practices have had a great influence on the way African Americans express themselves in worship. Because of this great influence of tradition, African-American worship is distinctive. It has a distinct history, tradition, and practice.

This book unfolds in the following sequence and explication of sub-headings:

- Chapter 1 gives an overview of Baptist history.
- Chapter 2 is an overview focusing on some significant milestones of African-American social history and its relationship to the Baptists.

- Chapter 3 examines some selected, distinctive traits of African-American worship: An overview of the socio-historical contexts and an explication of the key elements in worship.
- Chapter 4 looks at rituals, conversion, and ordinances.
- Chapter 5 highlights and discusses the elements of a sample of worship.
- Chapter 6 gives a summary of the book.

Chapter 1 focuses on Baptist history—a story full of struggles. When religious beliefs and practices represent major differences in the way people live their lives, those beliefs and practices can cause conflicts. The Baptists had to travel some rough roads to achieve their current level of freedom. During the 18th century, the struggle changed from the freedom of worship to the separation of church and state. During the 19th century, there was the issue of slavery. The Reconstruction Era (1865-1877) was a time of missionary activity. White missionaries were sent into the African-American community to establish schools and churches.

Chapter 2 provides an overview focusing on some significant milestones of African-American social history and its relationship to the Baptists. Africans were brought to America and held in bondage for more than 200 years. Africans were at a great disadvantage in America because of the life they were forced to live. Their freedom was taken away from them. The Baptist church was attractive to slaves because the preaching of the revival services offered them a vision of God's justice. Although there were scattered instances of African Americans holding membership in white churches, they did not have the same freedom as whites. The slavery problem created spiritual stresses and social tensions that led to the separate church movement among African-American Baptists.

Chapter 3 examines some selected, distinctive traits of African-American worship. It is important to understand that, unlike the white church, the African American church is a product of racism and was founded during the time of slavery. African Americans developed a unique faith peculiar to their social history. They accepted the white man's religion but changed it into a form with which they could identify and that met their needs. The African prayer life, preaching styles, and music will be surveyed to determine their influences on African-American people.

Chapter 4 looks at some rituals, conversion, and ordinances of African Americans and the African-American church. There are some rituals that began years ago, which some African Americans still practice today. The chapter deals with how the conversion experiences of African Americans have changed the lives of generations of African Americans. To African Americans, conversion is more than just the changing of habits. The ordinances are viewed from the African American's perspective, beginning with slavery.

Chapter 5 discusses the elements of a typical worship service, analyzing each act or element of the service.

Chapter 6 summarizes chapters 2 through 5 while focusing on some significant points and insights. Chapter 6 also looks at what has happened and is happening as a result of the data. As a result of this project, an important insight has been revealed. Once members of a given congregation are taught the fundamentals of their history and the place they hold in the larger society, they tend to become more responsive to the particulars of history. I believe the African-American Baptist Church will continue to be the place where one can experience a necessary bond with like-minded individuals.

In their struggles, the Baptists traveled some rough roads to achieve freedom, which they believed was necessary in order to worship God.

Baptists insisted upon believers' baptism; therefore, they refused to baptize their infants. This violated the requirements of the state church. Baptists also insisted on their right to worship in their own way and in their own churches. These beliefs caused friction between church and state.

During the early 18th century, the struggle for freedom changed from the freedom to worship to the separation of church and state. Baptists believed the church must not dictate to the state nor the state to the church. The Baptists believed the activity of the state in religious affairs would keep them from enjoying religious freedom. Early Baptists also organized what are known as associations. These associations created a wider fellowship of the congregations. The Baptist associations had no control over the beliefs and practices of member churches.

The 19th century provided another frontier for the question of religious liberty. There was the issue of slavery. African Americans could not have religious freedom as long as they were enslaved.

During the early 19th century, many of the white churches did not support the abolition of slavery. In fact, African Americans were the objects of missionary endeavors. Whites thought the best way to integrate African Americans into American society was through Christian experience.

During the Reconstruction Era, in an effort to meet the needs of African Americans, white missionaries were sent into the African-American community to start schools and churches, but African-American churches made it clear that what was needed among them was not outside leadership but opportunities and resources.

During the mid-19th century, there was an emergence of separate African-American churches. Although forbidden by law in many states, African-American churches had been organized as early as the late 1700s. Today, there are many Baptist conventions, congresses, associations, organizations, and churches.

PART ONE

An Overview of History

CHAPTER 1

An Overview of Baptist History

This writer's interest in this project emanates from his experience as an African-American Baptist preacher in the southern United States. The African-American Baptist Church is an American, black, cultured denomination within the mainstream of the United States, in that, it has evolved out of the Baptist tradition of Protestantism. Before discussing the concept of African-American worship as pertaining to its characteristics, it is necessary to present a brief historical overview of American Baptists.

Some Baptists maintain there has been a continuous succession of Baptist congregations since the time of John the Baptist, Jesus, and the apostles. Other Baptists cite the continental Anabaptists of the 16th century as the major progenitors of the Baptist movement. Despite these disagreements, most scholars now locate the origins of the Baptist movement among certain 17th-century British Puritans, who differed from other Puritans regarding two doctrinal points. The 17th-century British Puritans believed in baptism by immersion rather than by sprinkling and in baptizing adult believers rather than infants. Baptists believed these practices followed necessarily from their own Puritan interpretation of the New Testament, in which the true Church is a body of believers who have been regenerated and sanctified.[1]

Religious Liberty

One of the leaders who stood out during the 17th century was John Smyth, a young Cambridge graduate, who was a clergyman in the Church of England. John Smyth and his followers formed a church in Amsterdam in 1606. Not long after the establishment of this church by Smyth, a small group of Baptists, left Smyth and went with Thomas Ielwys, one of Smyth's close friends. Helwys and his followers established a church in London in 1611 or 1612.[2] The English Baptists grew and, later, were divided into conflicting groups: the General Baptists, who believed in a general redemption of all people, and the Particular Baptists, who believed Christ died for an elect few. The Baptist tradition has always taken freedom and autonomy seriously. The conflicts and divisions throughout history clearly demonstrate this point.

During this time, Baptists immigrated to America. The Baptist story in America begins with the work of Roger Williams, a young, English-born Puritan preacher who went to Boston, Massachusetts. While in Massachusetts, he became disgruntled about the fact that people were being deprived of their religious freedoms. He believed there should be a separation of church and state. Williams' beliefs led to conflicts resulting in him being exiled from the Massachusetts Colony. While in exile, he led a movement for the founding of the Rhode Island Colony in 1636. As a result of the founding of the Rhode Island Colony, the first Baptist church was organized in America in Providence.[3] In 1639, some Baptists newly arrived in Rhode Island and seeking refuge from religious oppression, influenced Williams to accept their view of the church. He became convinced their insistence upon adult conversion and a rejection of infant baptism provided the pattern for freeing the true Church from its Jewish antecedents.[4] Williams believed that one must be free to be able to worship God. To him, it seemed that worship must be sincere, and anything interfering with a person's freedom weakened his or her worship.

Small groups with Baptist convictions were in New Hampshire, Massachusetts, Connecticut, and Rhode Island. With the exception of Rhode Island, New England did not provide a congenial home for Baptists. On the contrary, Baptists were the victims of persecution. First, they insisted on believers' baptism and refused to baptize their infants, thus violating the requirements of the state church. In the second place, the Baptists insisted on their right to worship in their own way and in their own churches. Consequently, they resented the efforts of the state to curtail these rights. Finally, they insisted on the separation of church and state, a principle which had its best illustration in the work of Roger Williams.[5]

The Baptist movement continued to spread until groups surfaced throughout the colonies, their cause being aided by the evangelistic fervor of the Great Awakening.[6] Great Awakening is the name given to a series of religious revivals in the American Colonies during the 18th century. These revivals had a strong influence on religious life in America in that they emphasized individual religious experience, rather than the religious doctrines of a specific church.[7] Wherever Baptists went, they continued their struggle for religious liberty. As the movement for independence developed, it offered the Baptists an exceptional opportunity to set forth their position of religious freedom. Before and after the Revolution, they campaigned throughout America for freedom of religious belief and worship.[8]

The Baptist passion for religious liberty was born out of specific circumstances and definite convictions about religious experience. As individuals, and, later, as congregations of the 17th century studied the Scriptures, they arrived at tenable positions in matters of doctrine and practice and announced their faith to their respective communities. As a result, opposition set in. Like any other persecuted sect, Baptists struggled for the freedom to behave religiously as they pleased, to win new converts to their ranks, to gather groups together for worship, study, and discipline, and to publish their own views in printed form.[9]

Church and State

The struggle for freedom changed during the early 18th century from the freedom to worship to the separation of church and state.

> As emphasis was placed upon individual responsibility to God, men responded. Since the new charter granted to the Massachusetts Bay Colony in 1691 had guaranteed only religious toleration, and had not exempted Baptists from taxation for the support of the state church, they refused to pay on the principle that no man should be coerced to support another man's church. As a result, their property frequently was sold for tax costs, as at Ashfield, near Boston, where they suffered keenly.[10]

The belief was that the church must not dictate to the state nor the state to the church. The church must have the freedom to obey the Lord and carry out His will. Baptists believed the activity of the state in religious affairs would keep them from enjoying this religious liberty.

The efforts put forth by Baptists on behalf of religious freedom during and after the American Revolution contributed greatly, not only to the ultimate achievement of their goals, but also to their popularity. Indeed, the Revolution provided them with a unique opportunity. They had little to lose and much to gain. They were bound by no ties of loyalty to a state church in England. Their participation in the War of Independence was therefore a contribution to the cause of religious liberty.[11]

The ultimate safeguard for complete liberty in America was the adoption of a constitution, which included no religious test clause and plainly prevented the interference of the state in religion. The Virginia Baptists petitioned President Washington personally for such a safeguard to be written into the Federal Constitution. He promised to lend his support to such a move for religious liberty.

Even then, disestablishment did not come in Massachusetts until 1833 to mark the final triumph of a long struggle on behalf of religious freedom.[12]

Religious liberty was very important to the Baptists. For Baptists, that which is spiritual supersedes everything else. It was important to them to be able to worship as they desired and to exercise their faith without restrictions.

Associations

These early Baptists also emphasized the need for a wider fellowship of the congregations through membership in what were called associations. Associations were considered organizations confined to a certain area within a state. This was based not only upon expediency but also upon a conviction that such connectionalism was essential to express the church universal—a position clearly indicated in their early confessional statements. Their protection of the autonomy of each congregation with respect to its inner life was intended not to stress independence from other congregations, nor to disavow the reality of the larger church, but to recognize the Lordship of Christ over each congregation rightly organized and invested with the powers of a Gospel church.[13] The Baptist associations had no control over the beliefs and practices of member churches. Each church was a body of Christ in itself, and associational membership did not change its nature.

Missionary Movements

Priorities changed somewhat during the 18th century. Religious liberty became the freedom to create a Christian America and other Christian nations, as well, through the missionary enterprise. Jews, infidels, and barbarians were not to remain in their religious beliefs but were to be evangelized and set at liberty to follow their consciences and the leading of God's Spirit. As the 18th century evolved to the 19th, the issues associated with religious liberty took on global dimensions for the Baptist community.[14]

By 1825, Baptist missionaries from England and America had penetrated every continent against the stiffest odds and government restrictions prohibiting evangelism. For many, religious liberty had come to mean the right of the Baptists to propagate the faith in non-Christian cultures.[15]

Slavery

Meanwhile, in the United States, racial and ethnic realities provided another frontier for the question of religious liberty in the 19th century. That great libertarian, John Leland, had introduced a resolution in 1789 to the General Committee of the United Baptist Churches of Virginia calling for the abolition of slavery; but, four years later, after Leland left the state, the committee rescinded its action for political considerations. Leland had dared to carry the issue of religious liberty beyond the color barrier to the slave community as well when he wrote, "Liberty of conscience, in matters of religion, is the right of slaves beyond contradiction; and yet many masters and overseers will whip and torture the poor creatures for going to meetings, even at night, when the labor of the day is over."[16]

While Baptists in the North, South, and West did support the abolition of slavery before the Civil War, there is little evidence that religious liberty was a central concern. In fact, the black population—slave and free—was an object of domestic missionary endeavors. It was the hope and expectation of the white church that Christian experience, morality, and behavior would provide Afro-Americans with the best chance of any form of integration into American society.[17]

While the Southern Baptists concentrated on the Southern states' rights and economic solidarity, Baptists in the North and West redoubled their efforts to reach a variety of new constituencies. In 1834, as the Foreign Mission Society began its work in Europe, the American Baptist Home Mission Society inaugurated efforts among American immigrant groups. Leaders of the Home Society believed their evangelical task involved Americanization— making the immigrants become American in their habits and customs. The Home Society started numerous programs in education and new church development, which had as their unifying purpose the transformation of different cultural and social patterns. While immigrant leaders appreciated the funds and opportunities made possible by these efforts, the response was more often a reaction which led to separate, but cooperating, ethnically diverse conferences.[18]

African-American Churches

A similar, unpredicted reaction occurred among the black churches. During the Reconstruction Era, the American Baptist Home Mission Society took a special interest in the needs of the recently freed slaves and sent missionaries south to start schools and churches in the black community. While many positive results emanated from educational and evangelistic efforts, the black leaders recognized the fact that there were some very important needs of the black people which were not being met. They felt that the white educational literature the American Baptist Home Mission Society was providing to the black congregations was inadequate. The black leaders also saw the need for black leadership in an environment of continuing racism and segregation. This situation led to the idea of organizing black churches and missionary endeavors. By 1905, black Americans, for their own reasons, were among the loudest voices in support of religious freedom.[19]

However, whatever good intentions there were in the efforts of the American Baptist Home Mission Society, the reaction of the American immigrant groups and the black churches made it very clear that what was needed among them was not outside leadership but opportunities and resources. It was obvious that there were leaders in each group who could do a much better job than any outsider in continuing the already existing cultural and social patterns because they had the necessary experience and knew the needs of their particular ethnic group.

There was an emergence of separate black Baptist churches and organizations during the mid-19th century. Although forbidden by law in many states, black churches had been organized as early as 1778 in Georgia. In Boston, New York, and Philadelphia, similar churches were started in the early 1800s. In the South, such congregations were free-standing before emancipation; in the North and West, the black churches were invited to attend associational meetings and other society gatherings as cooperating members. The first black association was created among eight churches in Ohio in 1834. Like other Christian groups, white Baptists were not prepared for racial integration, even in the associational context, and black Baptists were forced to seek fellowship in mission involvement within their own organizational patterns. During the Reconstruction, this segregation became acute, and black Baptist leaders formed their own national mission societies.[20]

William Henry Brackney said, "Baptists as a whole continue to divide and conquer, sometimes even each other."[21] Today, there are many Baptist conventions, congresses, associations, organizations, and churches. There have been major divisions occurring within the Baptist denomination. Many of these divisions have been along regional, racial, and theological lines. Included in the major bodies of Baptists are

American Baptists, Southern Baptists, National Baptists of America (African American), National Baptists of the U.S.A. (African American), and Progressive National Baptists (also African American).

Summary

The Baptists story is full of struggling along rough roads to achieve the freedom they have at present. These struggles are driven by the belief that one must be free to be able to worship God.

Baptists insisted on believers' baptism; therefore, they refused to baptize their infants. This violated the requirements of the state church. Baptists also insisted upon their right to worship in their own way and in their own churches. These beliefs caused friction between church and state.

During the early 18th century, the struggle for freedom changed from the freedom to worship to the separation of church and state. Baptists believed the church must not dictate to the state nor the state to the church. The Baptists were of the belief that the participation of the state in religious affairs would keep them from enjoying this religious freedom.

These early Baptists also organized what have become known as associations. These associations created a wider fellowship of the congregations. The Baptist associations had no control over the beliefs and practices of member churches.

The 19th century provided another frontier for the question of religious liberty. There was the issue of slavery. Blacks could not have religious freedom as long as they were enslaved. During the early 19th century, many of the white churches did not support the abolition of slavery. In fact, blacks were the object of missionary endeavors. Whites thought the best way to integrate blacks into American society was through the Christian experience.

During the Reconstruction Era, in an effort to meet the needs of blacks, white missionaries were sent into the black community to start schools and churches, but the black churches made it clear that what was needed was not outside leadership but opportunities and resources.

During the mid-19th century, there was an emergence of separate black churches. Although forbidden by law in many states, black churches had been organized as early as the late 1700s. Today, there are many Baptist conventions, congresses, associations, organizations, and churches.

CHAPTER 2

African-American Social History and the Baptists

When I realized that I was in the real world, I was living in Turrell, Arkansas. When I was 7, my parents moved to Brownsville, Tennessee—a small town about 60 miles east of Memphis, Tennessee. In Brownsville, two important realities shaped my consciousness: the black church experience and the way white people treated blacks.

The black church introduced me to a religious experience that has followed me to this day. It gave me the spiritual foundation and strength to survive in a world of oppression and remain reasonably sane. At a Christian Methodist Episcopal church (C.M.E.), at a revival meeting, on a mourners' bench, I offered myself for membership at the age of 12. Every first and third Sunday, the members of that little country church would meet to experience the presence of God. The Spirit of God was present there to soothe the troubled minds of the black worshipers and give them hope. Through singing, praying, and preaching, God assured the black people in Brownsville, Tennessee, of His love and concern for their well-being.

There was also another experience in Brownsville that has not been erased from my memory. The white people in Brownsville made it clear they thought blacks were not equal to them in any way, shape, form, or fashion. Their beliefs were made clear by the way they treated the blacks. Black Americans in most cases, were treated as white people's servants and, in some cases, even slaves. Many of the whites in Brownsville called blacks "niggers." Most of the blacks in

Brownsville had to depend on the whites for survival. In most cases, blacks lived on farms and/or in houses belonging to white owners. Blacks, therefore, were expected to plow the fields, pick the cotton, and obey the rules of the white people.

Blacks were alright as long as they stayed in "their places," as defined and dictated by white people. Whites' rules meant attending separate schools, using secondhand school books already used by the white students for three or four years, going to the balcony when attending a movie, going to a back or side door of a restaurant to be given food, and drinking water from a fountain or using a restroom designated for "coloreds." The rules meant scratching at times when one did not itch and laughing when nothing was funny. They meant keeping one's mouth closed when called a nigger. Blacks had no name except their first name or "boy," "uncle," or "auntie" for those past the age of 60.

I recall one occasion when a white man came to the house where we lived and called out to whomever was inside. My mother went to the door to see who was calling. I, a young teenager at the time, followed her to the door. The white man said to my mother, "Hello auntie." I looked at my mother and said, "Mama, I did not know this man was some kin to you." My mother, with a frightened look on her face, turned and said, "Shut up, boy." My innocent reaction to what the white man had said frightened my mother because she knew what could happen as a result. She was afraid of white people because of her experience growing up in Mississippi. She had witnessed white people hanging blacks and/or burning them alive for no reason other than the fact they were black. The life of a black person was not easy in Brownsville. Many of the blacks were poor, and the whites who were in control saw to it they stayed that way. However, blacks made it because of their faith in the God who met them at church on Sunday mornings.

Along with many other things African Americans have had to endure in America was the fact that for many years, they were denied a past. African-American history was not taught in the public school systems. The standard portrayals of African Americans in textbooks reflected what might be called a Southern viewpoint. African Americans were portrayed as people who were less than Caucasian Americans in every way that Caucasian society deemed important. In his book, *God of the Oppressed*, the experience James H. Cone had in Bearden, Arkansas, unfortunately was not an isolated case in America. Cone said, "White people did everything within their power to define black reality, to tell us who we were—and their definition, of course, extended no further than their social, political, and economic interests."[1] African Americans were treated as if they either had developed a severe case of amnesia or they were not intelligent enough to know who they were. Of course, the idea was to define the actual existence of African Americans in a way that would give whites a feeling of superiority.

However, African Americans did not want to claim their "own" past. John Hope Franklin, in an essay in the book, *Africa and the Afro-American Experience*, said,

> Speaking before a Congress on Africa in Atlanta in 1895, the Honorable John C. Smyth, a former minister to Liberia, said that 'negroes are averse to the discussion of Africa, when their relationship with that ancient and mysterious land is made the subject of discourse or reflection.' More than a generation later, in 1937, the distinguished historian Dr. Carter G. Woodson said that 'Negroes themselves accept as compliment the theory of a complete cultural break with Africa, far above all things they do not care to be known as resembling in any way those 'terrible Africans.' Even Dr. W. E. B. DuBois, in his autobiography, *Dusk of Dawn*, wrote of Blacks 'who had inherited the fierce repugnance toward anything African, which was the natural result of the older colonization scheme...They felt themselves Americans, not Africans. They resented and feared any coupling with Africa.'[2]

Though these sentiments are still alive in some African Americans, they are in contrast to many views African Americans are expressing today. There is an increasing number of African Americans who feel the need to know more about African-American history and believe it is imperative that this formative information be made available. The sentiment is, if African Americans are to become what they are capable of becoming; are to reach the goals they are capable of reaching; are to increase their confidence and enhance their self-esteem, they must know more about who they were, as well as who they are.

The African and Slavery

"The relationship between African Americans and Africa was, of course first established by the African slave trade itself."[3] Therefore, any history of African Americans must begin in Africa.[4] Africa is the homeland of most of America's black population. Africans were brought to America because of a need for a stronger labor force. The native, Indian population had failed to deliver the necessary muscle force to clear the woods, build the cities, and, eventually, make cotton the productive crop that it was.[5] Africans were captured and brought to America against their will. They came under very dehumanizing conditions. As a result, they were considered property to be used for the benefit of their owners.

For 200 years, Africans were held in bondage in America. For two centuries, these human beings were systematically deprived of every right of personality. Racism was institutionalized, and the sacredness of the family was violated. Children were sold from their mothers, and fatherhood was made illegal.[6] Lerone Bennett, Jr. in his book, *Before the Mayflower*, said, "The Mississippi court ruled that the rape of a slave woman was an offense unknown to common or civil law. A Kentucky court ruled that the father of a slave was unknown to their law."[7]

Even though slaves were permitted to marry, the law did not recognize slave marriages. As a result, there was no conscious effort on the part of a master to keep a slave family together. In fact, any member of a family could be sold at any time to another master in another city, county, or state. At slave marriage ceremonies, preachers often would join couples until "death or distance do you part."[8]

Those who owned slaves could treat them in this manner and not be punished themselves because they were protected by law. This type of treatment was part of the system. Because slaves were considered to be property, the slave owners had control over their lives. They determined the destiny of many things occurring in the lives of black Americans. Racism was institutionalized; therefore, for whites to consider providing an atmosphere for blacks to be a part of a humanistic lifestyle was out of the question.

In his book, *The Negro in the Making of America*, Benjamin Quarles said it is difficult to try to generalize about the actual lot of a slave because slavery was really a dual system. Slavery was not only an economic way of life; it was also a system of racial adjustment. Whites used slavery as a regulating device when it came to black and white relationships. Whites felt that, if the blacks were set free, they would lower the whole character of society. Therefore, slavery was a means of keeping them under control.[9]

Quarles also points out that, in order to survive in a strange and cruel land, slaves had to make some adjustments. One type of adjustment involved the manner in which they communicated with whites. The slaves always were faced with the task of pleasing the masters. Therefore, when slaves talked to whites, they were very careful about what they said. They would listen to the masters' voices and determine what kind of response he or she wanted. Then, they would say the things the masters wanted to hear.[10] In order not to upset the masters and make life any more difficult than it already was, the slaves became actors and played roles to please the masters.

Walter Pitts, in his work, *Old Ship of Zion*, said there also was another type of adjustment for the Africans who were brought to America. Africans who were brought to America were not all from the same tribe but were put together as one in America. Each African tribe had its own set of customs. Therefore, there was the task of adjusting to the different tribal customs of African origin. The diverse African ethnic groups were able to make this adjustment without giving up their native beliefs. Each group was able to hold on to those ideas that were important to its survival.[11]

In order for the Africans of various tribal backgrounds to continue their religious practices, they had to steal away at night to some secret, secluded place where the overseers could not see or hear them. In these secret meetings, they could sing their songs and teach them to their children. The slave owners did not approve of these meetings; therefore, the Africans really were taking a great risk by holding them.[12] There was the risk of being punished for going against the will of the owner. Punishment was a way of trying to keep the slaves in line. "There was a general belief that African Americans were a childlike race and should be punished just as children."[13] Because of the importance of keeping these meetings a secret, these enslaved Africans invented codes and practices that owners and overseers did not understand. A favorite code used was usually a song, or spiritual, such as "Steal Away to Jesus," that told of such a meeting in words of double meaning.[14] The words of the song said, "Steal away to Jesus," but they also meant that it was time to steal away to that secret place where the slaves could be themselves, teach their children, and worship their God in a way that was comfortable to them. They were to slip away to a place where the master could not see or hear them.

Mechal Sobel makes a statement, in her work, *Trablin' On*, that further show the difficulty of the life of a slave. She said, "For the slave to become his best self he had to follow African standards, but to attain the most freedom of action he had to become a good slave."[15] This was a major conflict in the life of a slave. This was a dichotomy with which slaves were confronted. They were African, but also slaves; two thoughts, two opposed efforts.

In order to survive with a reasonable amount of sanity, slaves had to live in two worlds. They had to continue in the traditions and values set by their foreparents if they were to become their best selves. The African standards were the things that gave them self-esteem and made them feel like human beings. Yet, on the other hand, if they wanted to experience any freedom at all, they had to become good slaves; they had to be obedient to their masters. Their masters were not interested in maintaining the African standards; they only wanted slaves to be good slaves.

Baptists and Slavery

James Melvin Washington, in his book, *Frustrated Fellowship*, expresses some reasons why the Baptist church was attractive to slaves. Washington said slaves were permitted to attend revival services, and the preaching at these services offered them a vision of God's justice. They did not know when justice would take place, but it was something to anticipate eagerly. By allowing the slaves to demonstrate religious expressions, these revivals also helped the slaves to retain part of their own religious beliefs. Washington also said, "it provided a new source of psychic energy to help them meet the harsh challenge of the new world."[16]

Blacks were ready for the great awakenings of the revival services. They were looking for a more positive outlook than what they had. They had lost that sense of coherence they had enjoyed in their homeland. They were looking for new coherence and a new sense of unity and purpose. Therefore, the Baptist invitation came at a time when blacks were comfortable enough with spoken English to appreciate the Baptist message and uncomfortable enough with the life they were forced to live to hunger for a better one.[17]

Blacks first became Baptists during the first Great Awakening. Their presence at the revivals led to their conversions, or rebirths, and they began joining congregations. Blacks were expected to have personal experiences of rebirth; to recount these experiences publicly; to be considered by the whole congregation as candidates for baptism, and, if accepted, to be baptized in a symbolic drowning; to be blessed by a laying on of hands or to be given the right hand of fellowship; and to sign the covenant and join the congregation of the elect.[18]

Initially, white Baptist involvement in the evangelization of slaves was minimal. There were scattered instances of black Baptists holding membership in white churches. As early as 1772, Robert Steven and 18 other black Baptists held membership in the First Baptist Church of Providence, Rhode Island. By 1772, the First Baptist Church of Boston was receiving black Baptists in its membership.[19] Although blacks were received as members, they did not have the same freedoms as whites. They were members of the Baptist church, but they still were slaves. The question of slavery became a problem in the Baptist tradition. An example of this is mirrored in an 1802 report of the Dover Baptist Association in Virginia. Here, it was said that some churches admitted to their church meetings all male members, whether slave or free. Nevertheless, the report reflected a movement against this tendency.

> By experience this plan was found vastly inconvenient. The degraded state of the minds of the slaves, rendered them totally incompetent to the task of judging correctly respecting the business of the church, and in many churches there were a majority of slaves; in consequence of which great confusion

often arose. The circular letter argued and advised, that although all members were entitled to the privilege, yet that none but free male members should exercise any authority in the Church. The Association after some debate, sanctioned the plan by a large majority.[20]

Albert J. Raboteau, in his book, *Slave Religion*, said, "For slaves...to participate in the organization, leadership, and governance of church structures was perceived as imprudent; and attempts were made to carefully limit black participation."[21] Whites did not want blacks to have this type of authority. There was the fear of blacks gaining some independence and whites losing control of the blacks.[22]

Even though slaves held memberships in the Baptist church, they were not accorded the dignity and respect of equal participants in the Christian fellowship. Slaves did not have the same rights and privileges within the congregation as the white Baptists. Slaves were looked upon as people whose minds were not of the same quality as whites, which meant they were not able to think on the same level as whites. Because of this alleged mode of thinking, slaves were not able to express themselves in the white churches. Therefore, they were not permitted to be part of the decision-making processes of the church.

There were also black preachers who worked to evangelize the slaves, although being slaves themselves, they were limited in what they could do. Generally, they were not permitted to have their own churches. As a result, slaves would steal away to some secluded place and hold their own meetings, where they could be free to be themselves and worship God. Some of these slave preachers began to understand the Word of God in a different light. They saw more in God's Word than what the white preachers were telling them. Eventually, these slave preachers became increasingly aware of how dehumanizing white, Christian movements were to the Christian slave population. This new light led them to see their fellow slaves differently. They became closer to the slave community in order to create a new relationship with their brothers and sisters of Africa. As a result, there was a sense of belonging to a slave group that was distinct from that of the dominant group of Baptists.[23]

The antislavery movement created a problem for some whites. It caused them to have to make a decision between religious conscience and social responsibility. There were those who disliked slavery, but they were more concerned about white males and their rights as property owners than they were about freeing the slaves.[24]

Although white Baptists were slow to support the emancipation of slaves, they were strongly in favor of the emancipation of their souls from the bondage of sin. The idea of blacks being inherently equal to whites created a problem for them. This idea challenged their belief that slavery, rather than religion, was the most effective means of social control.[25] To give slaves their freedom would indicate that they were human and deserved to be treated as such and that they were in some way equal. Baptist equality preachers became aware of the fact that Christianity meant the loss of control, since they believed slavery was the most effective means of social control.

The slavery problem created spiritual stresses and social tensions leading to the separate church movement among black Baptists. One historian said, "Separate churches could not have been born during slavery if nobody had become dissatisfied with their religious experiences in white churches."[26] This movement was really a sign of rebelliousness against white oppression and institutional racism. Among the basic beliefs of Baptists were the ideas of the church as a regenerated membership, baptism by immersion, the authority of Scripture with the New Testament as a guide of faith and practice, the autonomy of the local church, the separation of church and state, and the equality of believers. In his book, *A History of Black Baptists*, Leroy Fitts said, concerning these Baptist principles,

> To be sure, many white Baptists never sought to apply most of these basic principles to their black membership. In fact, such principles were at variance to the "peculiar institution" of slavery. . . . Yet, the failure to apply basic Baptist principles led to the fertilization of the ovum for the birth of an independent or separate church movement among black Baptists.[27]

This type of non-Christian treatment of black people in what was supposed to be a Christian setting is what drove blacks to separate and form their own churches. It was not because they did not want to be with white people, but because of the way they were treated by white people.

Between 1788 and 1834, black Baptists formed their first consciously black Baptist congregations and supported the rise of the major black Baptist leaders who formed associations. Associations were considered organizations confined to a certain area within a state. These leaders argued for the formation of these associations for the purpose of engaging in missionary work beyond the local congregations.[28] The first black association was created among eight churches in Ohio in 1834. White Baptists were not ready for racial integration, even on the associational level. As a result, black Baptists were forced to seek fellowship in mission involvement within their own organizational patterns.[29] "But more was at stake than the fulfillment of the missionary dream to save the world for Christ."[30] There was also the issue of religious freedom, which black Baptist congregations acquired between 1788 and 1831.[31]

The forming of associations led to even wider cooperative movements. The black leaders saw the need for the various associations to unite in a spirit of cooperation. For that reason, associations developed cooperative programs leading to the organization of state conventions. The black Baptists of North Carolina were the first to bring the vision of cooperative associational programs to fruition with the organization of the General Baptist State Convention in 1866.[32] During Reconstruction, segregation became such a problem that black Baptist leaders formed, first, their own national mission societies and, later, a national convention, in 1886.[33] However, unity on a national level was not realized until 1895 when the National Baptist Convention of the United States of America was organized. This convention eventually split as a result of a dispute over the ownership and control of the Publishing Board. Consequently, the National Baptist Convention of America was organized. The new body was originally called the National Baptist Convention, Unincorporated. The last split occurred in 1961 when the Progressive National Baptist Convention was organized.[34]

Blacks were taken from their native land and brought to a strange land, made slaves, and planted in a racist society to be treated as less than human. As a result, they have been forced to swim against the current of life. Holding on to their existence has been a struggle.

In his book, *The Souls of Black Folk*, W. E. B. DuBois talks about the struggle of blacks. DuBois said, "It is a peculiar sensation, this double-consciousness, the sense of always looking at one's self through the eyes of others, of measuring one's soul by the tape of a world that looks on in amused contempt and pity."[35]

The struggle DuBois talked about has followed blacks through the centuries and is still alive. Its force may have changed somewhat, but no one has been able to say, "earth to earth, ashes to ashes, dust to dust," and walk away and leave it in some grave to decay.

Even in the midst of such a struggle, blacks have been able to hold on to a reasonable portion of sanity by holding on to the black church. For blacks, the church is the place to go to find peace and comfort, to unload troubles, and to load up with enough hope to last until another meeting time. It has been what James H. Evans, Jr. speaks about as being community.

In Evans' book, *We Have Been Believers*, he cites J. Deotis Roberts, who is quoted as having said, "We are persons-in-community. Our wholeness as persons depends upon a healthy group life in families, communities, and nations."[36]

In a speech made to the Associacao Nacional Casa Dandara International Seminar in Brazil in 1995, Alton B. Pollard III talked about community existing in the societies of Africa. He said,

> In the societies of Africa now physically removed, 'to be' was still 'to belong.' The individual existed (and often exists still) corporately in terms of the family, clan and whole ethnic group. Identity was grounded in a strong sense of community, in which individuals understood themselves as part of a people and where no person could live in isolation, materially or spiritually.[37]

The black church has been that place where one could go and find community, togetherness, and family environment—a place where one could experience the necessary bond with like-minded others. In the words of John S. Mbiti,

> Only in terms of other people does the individual become conscious of his own being, his own duties, his privileges and responsibilities towards himself and towards other people. The individual can only say 'I am, because we are; and because we are, therefore, I am.'[38]

Though there have been problems along the way, internal and external, the black church has become an energetic force in the advancement of the Christian faith.

Summary

Africans were taken from their native land and brought to America and held in bondage for 200 years. White Americans owned these Africans, who were brought to America against their will. The masters treated these African Americans as less than human, and the law protected the masters. The slave owners were protected because the slaves were considered their property. Therefore, the slave owners determined the destiny of many things occurring in the lives of African Americans.

As a means of survival in a strange and cruel land, slaves had to make some adjustments. One type of adjustment was the manner in which they communicated with whites. The slaves would say the things the master wanted to hear. This was done in order not to upset the master or make life any more difficult than it already was.

Because Africans who were brought to America were not all of the same tribe, there was the task of adjusting to the different tribal customs of African origin. In order for the Africans of various tribal backgrounds to continue their religious practices, they had to steal away at night to secret places.

The Baptist church was attractive to slaves because the preaching at the revival services offered them a vision of God's justice. The Baptist invitation came at a time when the slaves were uncomfortable enough with the life they were forced to live to hunger for a better one.

There were scattered instances of blacks holding membership in white churches. Although blacks were received as members, they did not have the same freedoms as whites. They were not allowed to participate in the Christian fellowship on an equal basis. For the Baptists, equality meant the loss of control, because they believed slavery was the most effective means of social control.

The slavery problem created spiritual stresses and social tensions leading to the separate church movement among black Baptists. The forming of associations led to even wider cooperative movements. Associations developed cooperative programs leading to the organization of state conventions. Black Baptists leaders formed their first national convention in 1886.

PART TWO

Worship

CHAPTER 3

Selected Distinctive Traits of African-American Worship

The following discussion on African-American worship is not intended to imply the practice of worship is exclusively applicable to a particular group or race, or that African American worship is better or worse than any other group or race. However, it is an attempt to deal with the reality that there are African-American churches and Caucasian churches. There are no signs like those that were posted by Caucasians on restrooms, water fountains, and other places in the '50s and '60s saying, "white only," or "colored." Yet, on Sunday mornings, many African Americans still look for churches whose parishioners are predominantly African American, and many Caucasians look for churches whose parishioners are predominantly Caucasian. The following discussion is an attempt to point out that the nature of Christian worship in the African-American church is different from the Caucasian church.

Melva Wilson Costen, in her work, *African American Christian Worship*, says African Americans share a common history reaching back to the African soil. Costen continues by saying African Americans were brought from Africa against their will, enslaved, and treated as less than human by those who were responsible for bringing them to America. This history created a need for communities of refuge, a hiding place "conducive to authentic communication with God and with one another."[1]

There is a vast difference in the histories of African Americans and Caucasians. Unlike the Caucasian church, the

African-American church is a product of racism and was founded during the time of slavery. African Americans were the "oppressed," while Caucasians were the "oppressors." African Americans were the "have-nots," while Caucasians were the "haves." The African-American church was created out of an environment that was totally different from the Caucasian church. In order to be free, African Americans had to find secret places to express themselves in worship. Even though African Americans were enslaved physically, they refused to be enslaved spiritually. Freedom was found through fellowshipping with one another and the ability to worship God in the manner in which they were accustomed and in a way that met their needs.

This writer agrees with Wyatt Tee Walker, who said in his book, *The Soul of Black Worship*, that African-American worship is different from Caucasian folks' worship. Walker continues by saying, "The root of this difference is in our peculiar social history."[2]

John E. Brandon in an article in the book, *The Black Christian Worship Experience*, says,

> The way blacks worship is determined on the basis of how blacks see and respond to God. This makes it a theological matter. Therefore, when we speak of the differences in worship of the black church from that of the white church, we are really pointing out a disparity in the perception of, and response to, God in history, the present moment, and what He promises for the future.[3]

Generally, when African-American congregations gather for worship, because of their social history, they see God as the One who was with Daniel in the lions' den, (Daniel 6); the Hebrew boys in the fiery furnace, (Daniel 3); their foreparents in slavery; and who has been with them in the midst of a racist society and brought them to the present moment. Their perception of God, in history and the present, gives them the courage to lean on His promises for the future. Therefore, the religion of African Americans is really a theology of hope. They have hope for the future, based on what God has done in the past and is doing in the present. This is not to say that Caucasian congregations do not have some type of hope in God, but those congregations, in general, cannot be at the same point with their theological interpretation of the acts of God because of the vast difference in their historical roots.

C. Eric Lincoln says in the foreword of *Black Religion and Black Radicalism* by Gayraud S. Wilmore,

> The blacks brought their religion with them. After a time they accepted the white man's religion, but they have not always expressed it in the white man's way. It became the blacks' purpose—perhaps destiny—to shape, to fashion, to re-create the religion offered them by the Christian slavemaster, to remold it nearer to their own peculiar needs. The black religious experience is something more than a black patina on a white happening. It is a unique response to a historical occurrence that can never be replicated for any other people in America.

This peculiar social history of African Americans produced a distinctive religious experience. Because of this history, African Americans had needs peculiar to themselves. Because their needs were different, they needed a religion that was different. Therefore, they accepted the Caucasian man's religion but changed it into a form with which they could identify.

This transformation was not an easy task. There were times when the slaves actually risked their lives in an effort to develop a worship life of their own. In an effort to find freedom, to understand the biblical message, and to express their own beliefs in response to almighty God, slaves had to find secret places in which to worship.

In secret places, the slaves were able to transform the Christianity given to them in America into a Christianity that met their needs. As a result, a unique, African-American faith was developed. This unique Christian faith gave them the assurance that there was deliverance from their oppression and hope for the future. The foundation of hope for the slaves was the life of the biblical Jesus. The slaves learned in those secret gatherings that Jesus also was despised, mistreated, and put to death. There was hope in the fact Jesus defeated all earthly oppression, assured in His resurrection, ascension, and promise of peace.[5] They saw in their own lineage and heritage a type of despisement, mistreatment, pain, and even death. There was an identification in experience that went deep into their hearts. Jesus suffered and died, and they also were suffering and dying.

In His suffering, they could see their own miseries. They entered into the fellowship of His suffering so that they could identify with the life of Jesus. This gave the slaves hope for a better tomorrow. Even though Jesus suffered, He came out victorious. Even though Jesus was misused, beaten, killed, and buried, there was a resurrection; Jesus got up. The slaves were down, but Jesus gave them hope of getting up.

Slave owners were not going to give African Americans a message of freedom, defeating their purpose. They wanted slaves, in every sense of the word, not free people. They wanted people who were bound, not who had a hope of being delivered. Therefore, they did not tell African Americans that Jesus suffered as they were suffering. They did not tell slaves that Jesus was born of poor parentage. Slaves were not told that Jesus' parents were so poor they could not offer even a lamb for the sacrifice, but instead had to offer doves. This part of the life of Jesus was omitted because the masters knew it was dangerous to inform the slaves that the life and teachings of Jesus meant freedom.

The enslaved worshipers found the necessary freedom in the secret places where they could hear an anticipated message of hope in God's Word. The community could experience divine freedom.[6] Their masters allowed them to hear sermons, but the sermons were without hope for African

Americans. The messages were designed to hold the slaves down, not lift them up; to keep them bound, not give them freedom in this world or the next. Albert J. Raboteau, in his work, *Slave Religion*, said, "Slaves frequently were moved to hold their own religious meetings out of disgust for the vitiated Gospel preached by their masters' preachers. Sermons urging slaves to be obedient and docile were repeated ad nauseam."[7] Raboteau continued by quoting a former slave who paraphrased the type of sermon to which he and other slaves constantly were subjected: "You slaves will go to heaven if you are good, but don't ever think you will be close to your mistress and master. No! No! There will be a wall between you; but there will be holes in it that will permit you to look out and see your mistress when she passes by. If you want to sit behind this wall, you must do the language of the text, 'Obey your masters.'"[8]

In the invisible institution of the African-American church the notion that God had meant for them to be slaves was dispelled. That invisible institution became an extended family to those who were left without a family because of the cruelty and insensitivity of slavery.

Therefore, worship in the African-American experience is the visible acting out of what African Americans believe about God based on their history. It is a worship experience that includes a black theology. Worship in the African-American church and African-American life cannot be separated. The expressions in worship are the result of what has happened and is happening in life. African Americans, through their creativity, were able to take an unfamiliar religion and worship experience and transform them to meet their needs. This transformation by no means diluted the true meaning of worship.[9]

John S. Mbiti, in his book, *Introduction to African Religion*, said, "Worship is a means of renewing contact between people and God, or between people and the invisible world."[10]

People perform acts of worship to keep this contact alive between themselves and God.

According to William Nicholls, in his book, *Jacob's Ladder,* "Worship as most people know is, 'worthship.' To give worship to anyone is to accord them due recognition of their inherent dignity and value, of their worth or worthiness."[11]

There is no substantial evidence that the dramatic representation of the great themes of the Christian story, as told in the black worship experience, are any less potent and powerful than they are in any other worship experience.[12] African-American worship is Christian worship. African Americans recognize the events of Christianity. When they gather to worship, they renew contact with God, attribute praise, honor, and proper recognition to Him. They revere and honor Him. They use the Bible as their guide, but because of the social history of African Americans, the nature of worship is different.

Raboteau said, "Slaves, forbidden by masters to attend church, in some cases, even to pray, risked floggings to attend secret gatherings to worship God."[13] Raboteau goes on to say these secret meetings were important because they provided the slave community an opportunity to fashion its self-image as well as help individuals shape their self-images. The things that helped the slaves shape their self-images were their own experiences, symbols, values, and stories they had learned from their ancestors. They risked their lives in an effort to discover for themselves who they were and their rightful place in the universe. They had a negative image given to them by their oppressors. They lived in an environment which treated them as less than human. They were well aware of who the slave owners said they were and where those people said their places were, but they realized something was wrong with the information. Therefore, it was important for them to affirm their own self-worth and the worth of others. They needed a self-image that would give them a sense of a positive self. The only way to accomplish this was to gather in secret places, where they could lean on their own experiences, revisit those things that had been handed down from generation to generation, and where the masters could not control their worship of God.[14]

Even today, self-image is one of the main motivations of African-American worship. African Americans attend worship looking for something to give them a positive sense of self. Many come wounded and empty, looking for healing and wholeness. They come looking for a God who will listen to their problems and respond to their needs, who will lift them above the troubles of this world and give them hope for a better day, who will give them the affirmation of importance in His sight. The African-American church is an extended family for many African Americans. They come looking for someone to love them, nurturing, something that will fill the voids in their lives and give them a feeling of wholeness.

African Americans attend worship also to give praise and thanksgiving to God. In his book, *The Dynamics of Black Worship*, Edward P. Wimberly said the slaves risked worshiping to praise a God whom they knew had responded to and would respond to their needs.[15] Wimberly goes on by giving a definition of worship. He said worship is the response of praise, adoration, and reverence to God, who enters the lives of African Americans and brings meaning, healing, sustenance, and wholeness.[16] Thanksgiving is a major part of the prayers of African Americans. Their prayers thank God for all His blessings, including material possessions, protection, deliverance, and being with them throughout life's journey.[17]

Praise and thanksgiving are really at the top of the list when African Americans gather for worship. African Americans come together to affirm God's providence and power. They gather with the belief God, in Jesus Christ, is working for their good in every situation.

Prayer

In his work, *The Prayer Tradition of Black People*, Harold A. Carter said, "The African religious tradition has left many traces of its native influence on the lifestyle of black people in America. One of these basic influences has been the habit and impact of prayer."[18]

Carter goes on to point out that, in a quest for meaning and personhood of life, the basic African religious background revealed itself in the religious practices of African-American slaves.[19]

In his work, *Introduction to African Religion*, John S. Mbiti said prayer is found in all African societies and is the most common method of approaching God.[20]

Subject and Contents of Prayer

When the people of Africa prayed, their main focus was on the necessities of life. Because they traditionally have lived close to the land, in their prayers, they talked to God about rain, fertility, and welfare of humans, cattle, and fields. When praying, the slaves did not "beat around the bush" about their petitions but got to the point. They prayed for health, healing, protection from danger, safety in travelling, security, prosperity, preservation of life, peace, rain, the acceptance of sacrifices and offerings, and fertility for people, animals and crops.[21] These areas touched the basic needs of life. These were the areas of survival. Africans recognize God as the One who makes the sun rise and set, the rain fall, the mountains quake, and the rivers overflow. He is the One who heals the sick, helps the barren, and aids those in distress.[22]

Wyatt Tee Walker, in his work, *The Soul of Black Worship*, said,

> The subject and content of Black people's praying was (is) set by the social conditions that surround us. The prayers of our antebellum ancestors evidence an insatiable appetite for freedom (political liberation). The sociological circumstance directly

influenced the construction of the prayer utterances, then and now."23 Praying for the necessities of life is still prevalent with many African Americans today. God is viewed as a Father who is able to supply the needs of His children.

Places of Prayer

Moreover, Carter said, in the life of the slaves, prayers were born in the field. They spent most of their daylight hours in the field. Most of their prayers were for freedom and for their children to see a better day.[24]

Carter also said that many slaves had special places where they went to pray. Many had special spots or trees by rivers where God's presence was felt.[25] Time has not erased from memory the prayer habits of my stepfather, "Papa." Papa died in November of 1994 at the age of 108. He was a steward in a Christian Methodist Episcopal church for a while and then a deacon in a Baptist church. Papa had his special place, where he would go to pray at times. He was a farmer who lived on a farm he did not own. He was a share-cropper. Every spring, he would go down to a thicket about a quarter of a mile from the house where we lived. There, he would ask God for the health and strength needed to work the fields and for the necessary rain and sunshine that would result in a prosperous harvest so he would be able to feed and clothe his family. In the fall, after the crops were harvested and he had settled up with the farm's owner and purchased food and clothes for his family, he would go back to the thicket to thank God for answering his prayers. One of the favorite lines in Papa's prayer language was, "Thank you, Lord, for allowing me to be in a Gospel land and Bible country, where I can pick and choose my own praying ground." This thicket was Papa's special praying ground, special to him because he could feel God's presence there.

Papa did not go to this thicket every time he prayed, only at special times. He always prayed at night before going to bed and each morning when he got up. These prayers were prayed while on his knees beside his bed. The thicket was used for occasions more stressful than daily routines.

"The prayer tradition of contemporary African-American worship, rooted in Africa, has been nurtured in meeting houses and personal prayer lives of slaves and remains a means of vital force for spiritual release and fulfillment."[26]

Times of Prayer

Special "prayer and praise" times that establish the momentum for worship have continued without interruption from the invisible institution and praise houses in some congregations, particularly Baptists. Special times for prayer have been reinstituted recently as part of the recovery of the Black tradition.[27]

Prayer is one of the main events in today's worship. In many African-American worship services, when a person is called on to pray, the person speaks to God while other members of the congregation give affirmation by responding with such words as, "Yes, Lord," "say your prayers," and, "Amen," etc. In a call-and-response fashion, the congregation prays along with the person leading the prayer.

Many African-American congregations hold the view that it takes prayer to heat up things for worship. In many African-American congregations, the first item in the order of the worship service is what is called the "devotional service." As soon as Sunday school is over and after the deacons and pastor have met for prayer, the deacons usually make their way to the sanctuary to start the devotional service. The devotional service is an informal service where the deacons normally will assemble at the front of the sanctuary. They will lead the congregation in hymns, prayers, and testimonies. In some cases, no musical instruments are used. The only music is made by the clapping of the hands and patting of the feet. The main purpose of the devotional service is to heat things up for worship. There was a deacon in the congregation of which I am pastor who would stand before the people and say, "Come on you all, join in and let us get things hot for the pastor, so he will not have to work so hard." The main desire was to get the people "fired up" for worship and prepared to receive the Word of God.

There is also the mid-week prayer and testimony service. It is a belief among some of the older African Americans that no one should miss the mid-week prayer and testimony service because that is where one gets his/her "mid-week spiritual meal." The idea is that just coming to worship on Sunday will not keep one spiritually strong until the next Sunday. Therefore, to remain strong, one must eat of the "mid-week meal."

The mid-week prayer and testimony service consists of three major elements. The average service consists of singing, praying, and testifying. The singing of hymns, spirituals, or gospel songs are interweaved between the prayers and testimonies of the saints. The singing is like spiritual glue holding the service together.

There is also a prayer meeting held on New Year's Eve, known as "watch-night service." There is a spiritual belief among African Americans that a good ending of the old year and a good beginning of the New Year are necessary ingredients for the Christian's year.[28] Therefore, Christians come together to thank God for keeping them through the past year, to ask God's forgiveness for their sins, and to promise God and those assembled they will live holier lives during the new year.

Preaching

There was a question imbedded in the souls of the slaves and that is still asked by African-American worshipers today. The slaves wanted to know, "Is there a word from the Lord?" They were looking for the African-American preacher to deliver that word.[29] This expectation has not changed in the

African-American Christian community. Out of all the things that may occur during the worship service, preaching is considered the most important. Preaching is considered the center of the worship service. African-American Christians believe the African-American preacher should meet with God during the week and receive a message to be delivered to them. In the words of a man who was the chairman of a board of deacons for 40 years: "Pastor, we want to hear from heaven this morning."

Therefore, when the worshipers come to church on Sunday morning, they come expecting some good news from the Lord. The African-American preacher is expected to take the message from the Lord and make it come alive in the presence of the worshipers. The preacher is expected to tell the story in a manner that speaks to the needs of the worshipers. Those who come to worship want to be reassured that, in the midst of their individual situations, the Lord will make a way somehow.

Wyatt Tee Walker points out that the "roots and soil" of the African-American preaching phenomenon is the oral tradition of Mother Africa.[30]

In his work, *Black Preaching*, Henry Mitchell said the distinctiveness of preaching in the African-American religious community is a result of interweaving the Christian Gospel, men caught up in the black experience of slavery, oppression, and the African culture and folkways. Mitchell goes on to point out that, from this mixture, the African-American fathers developed an African-American religious tradition. In the African-American religious tradition were African-American culture sermons and the ways African-American men delivered and responded to them.[31]

The Preaching Style

Style is the vehicle which carries the message of God in the context of worship of a people conditioned by a struggle for freedom. Style is the way in which manner, method, word, tone, and feeling are appropriated in African-American preaching.[32] J. Alfred Smith said, "Style is the manner in which a speaker uses language in expressing thought...Style is the uniqueness of the thought and thought forms of the preacher. The personality, natural mental gifts, training, and cultural tastes are components which constitute style."[33]

A variety of preaching styles are utilized in African-American worship. These different styles in no way negate the traditional preaching heritage. African-American preaching is an artform based on a person's gifts and abilities. The African-American preacher must take words that were written many years ago and have been read by many of the people who are listening to the sermon and perform them with so much skill and intensity that they come alive in the presence of the hearers. It is not just the words, but it is how the words are presented.

The African-American preacher is able to be free in the pulpit, as long as the freedom is presented in a sincere manner. The worshipers in African-American congregations enjoy the freedom expressed by African-American preachers when they are preaching the Word of God.

Call-and-Response

One characteristic of the African-American preaching style is what is known as call-and-response. I have been a part of the call-and-response religious heritage since boyhood. I grew up in churches where call-and-response was an essential part of the worship service. The congregation was expected to be involved in the delivery of the message.

The call-and-response occurs when there is a dialogue between the preacher and the congregation. "If the black preaching tradition is unique, the uniqueness depends in part upon the uniqueness of the black congregation which talks back to the preacher as a normal part of the pattern of worship."[34] This dialogue has a tendency to bring the best out of the preacher in the proclamation of the Gospel. This is a style that will not work with all congregations because each must be willing to give a response to the preacher's call. The call-and-response style depends on the preacher and the personality of the congregation.

Mitchell also said, "To many whites and white-minded Negroes, the dialogue between preacher and congregation has been viewed as, at best, a quaint overreaction of superstitious simple folk, or an exuberant, childish expression of a beautiful, childlike faith such as could never occur in truly sophisticated Christian worship."[35] Mitchell then goes on to point out that few of any race could deny the fact that in call-and-response, the spiritual dialogue actually enhances their own powers of proclamation.[36] There are preachers who would welcome such support from the congregation. Some African-American preachers feel such a desire for this type of response from the congregation that they will ask for it, although they do not always receive it. They will pause and make such statements as, "Are you praying with me?" "Somebody ought to say, 'Amen!'" "Can I get a witness?" or "Somebody ought to know what I am talking about!" When there is a sincere dialogue between the African-American preacher and the congregation, there is a special fellowship. It is almost like singing a song with all parts blending. It creates harmony and causes the congregation to listen more attentively.

The call-and-response is not always an automatic occurrence, even in the congregations where this is accepted. In some congregations where the call-and-response is accepted, it will occur only when the preacher talks about something with which the people can identify, something relevant to their lives. The people respond because they understand what the preacher is preaching about. This understanding makes them interested in what the preacher is saying.

In the church where I pastor, for years, there was a deacon who encouraged members to attend Bible study and Sunday school for the purpose of learning as much as they could about God's Word. So, when the pastor stood to preach on Sunday mornings, the people knew what the preacher was talking about and, as a result, would be able to give support to the proclamation of the Gospel by saying, "Amen," or some other words of verbal response. When the congregation is responsive to the message, there is an experience of harmony with Jesus and one another as they come together to help proclaim and celebrate the Good News God has given the preacher.

Spontaneity

Spontaneity is another element in the African-American preaching style. Many African Americans prepare their sermons like a newscaster prepares the news report. They use all the information available at the time, but, many times, when the newscaster gets on the set, some late-breaking news will intrude. When late-breaking news comes in, it is inserted into the prepared manuscript. So, like a newscaster, many African-American preachers will insert late-breaking divine announcements into the prepared manuscript.[37]

The African-American sermon is not complete just because the preacher is in the pulpit and ready to deliver it. In many cases, the African-American preacher is preparing the sermon even while it is being preached. When preparing a sermon, a preacher may use all the information available at the time, but, often, other information is revealed during the time of delivery and is inserted. The African-American preacher believes in leaving room for the intervention of the Holy Spirit. Spontaneity has a way of inspiring the congregation. Sermon preparation is really in process until the benediction. African-American preachers do not allow manuscripts to turn them into slaves. These preachers have the freedom to express themselves according to the leadership of the Holy Spirit.

Chanting and Cadence

Another highlighting characteristic in African-American preaching is chanting or cadence. "The chanted sermon is as much a staple of African-American culture as spirituals, gospel, blues, and tales."[38] Chanting, in African-American preaching, has to do with intentional timing in the use of words, phrases, and sentences.[39]

There are many influences and sermons contributing to the development of the chanted sermon. The origins of this tradition can be found in the evangelical revivals of the mid-18th century, the ecstatic behavior encouraged by the revivals, the musical "tuned" voice of early Baptist preachers, and the pattern familiarized by the custom of lining-out hymns.[40]

The chanted sermon is a sermon composed on the spot in rhythmic, metrical speech. The meter is not based on accent, but on timing or the length of time between regular beats.[41] The preacher normally will start preaching in a normal, conversational voice, but, as the sermon progresses, the preacher speaks more rapidly. As the pace begins to increase, there is a chanting of the words in time to a regular beat. Sometimes, the preacher will lengthen vowels or rush together words in order to make a line match the meter. The regularity of the beat is accentuated by the preacher's gasp for air at the end of each line. The congregational responses— "Preach it, preach it," "Amen," "Yes," "Go ahead!"—reinforce the beat and simultaneously fill in the space left by the preacher's pause for breath.[42] In his book, *A Fire in the Bones*, Albert J. Raboteau, said,

> Congregational response is crucial to the delivery of the sermon. If response is weak or irregular, it will keep the preacher off stride. Conversely, if the preacher's sense of timing is poor, he will fail to rouse the congregation, and the sermon will fail.

There is, then, a reciprocal relation between preacher and congregation in the composition of the sermon. Ideally, the preacher's delivery will ignite the congregation's vocal response, which will, in turn, support and push him further.[43]

Intonation

Another characteristic of African-American preaching is intonation. There is a style of preaching common among African-American preachers known in some circles as "Whooping." "Whooping" is a sing-song style of preaching. Usually, a preacher will use it only in the conclusion of the sermon, although there are some who will use it in other parts of the sermon as a way of emphasizing certain points. Henry Mitchell said, "Others, often less well-educated and therefore less inhibited, tend to use some degree of tone throughout the message.[44]

"Historically speaking, intonation as a factor in black preaching style no doubt stems from the African custom of singing almost everything. The history of much of black Africa was preserved, in the absence of writing, in song.[45] It automatically makes some folks happy just to hear this aspect of their mother tongue sounded in the pulpit."[46] Some folks, even though they are being inspired by the sermon, by the mere fact they believe it to be the Word of God, will sit in anticipation of hearing the preacher whoop.

In some circles, "whooping" is referred to as the "gravy." There are those who say, "After you give me the meat of the sermon, put some gravy on it." They want the sermon to end on a high note with a special tone.

Mannerisms

African-American preachers are also known for exhibiting unusual mannerisms. They freely express themselves with behaviors unrelated to the message. "They add interest and signal a freedom and authentic personhood in which the congregation participates vicariously."[47] Some will unbutton their collar at a certain point in their message. Some will pull on their suspenders. Some will stare at the congregation, without saying a word, for a certain period of time. In his book, *The Hum*, Evans E. Crawford, said,

> Perhaps no preacher in recent memory embodied silence better than Howard Thurman, the former Dean of Rankin Chapel at Howard University, Washington, D.C., and Marsh Chapel, Boston, Massachusetts...Nobody made use of the pause like Howard Thurman. Students who have traveled hundreds of miles to hear him speak have been known to call him great just for rising, standing at the pulpit or podium, rubbing his hands over his face, and looking skyward before uttering his first word. His pauses initially seemed to embody what speakers call 'the dramatic pause.' Yet the pause for which he is well known seems to go beyond the merely dramatic. The spells of silence that were a part of his speaking are related more to meditation, and are best called 'meditative pauses' given what went before and after them.[48]

The self-contained, conversational tone of some Caucasian preachers cannot be maintained by African-American preachers who are caught up in doing God's preaching.[49] African-American preachers, who are mindful of the social history of African Americans and their present condition, have to be free to express their innermost feelings. African-American preachers feel what they are preaching about. African-American preaching is disciplined by life itself.

Singing

The religious music of African-American Christians came out of slavery. In his book, *The Souls of Black Folk*, W. E. B. DuBois, asserts,

> The music of Negro religion is that plaintive rhythmic melody, with its touching minor cadences, which, despite caricature and defilement, still remains the most original and beautiful expression of human life and longing yet born on American soil. Sprung from the African forests, where its counterpart can still

be heard, it was adapted, changed, and intensified by the tragic soul-life of the slave, until, under the stress of law and whip, it became the one true expression of a people's sorrow, despair, and hope.[50]

The music in the African-American religious experience reflects the history of the pilgrimage of African Americans. In the words of the songs, a portion of their story is told. African-American music reveals their sorrow, joy, despair, hope, frustration, and fulfillment. It reflects the theology of the journey of African-American people. It points out the very soul and substance of the African-American experience.[51]

"No matter what happened to African Americans, how bitter their portion, those African Americans who trusted in the Lord, never stopped singing the Lord's song in a strange land."[52] "Music was the common denominator allowing slaves brought to the New World to communicate in the language of one spirit. It was the form of their yearnings and hopes."[53]

Since the 17th century, African Americans have participated in two culturally distinct religious traditions. One tradition represents those African Americans who associated with Caucasian Protestant denominations. The second tradition was independently developed by Africans Americans who used the religious experience and practices brought with them from West Africa. The differences in these two traditions can be recognized by beliefs, worship styles, and the type of music used. The African-American congregations associated with the Caucasian Protestant denominations accepted their doctrines and obtained their musical repertoire from official hymnals, which included psalms, hymns, and spiritual songs. On the other hand, in the churches whose religious beliefs were distinctively African American, the musical repertoire consisted of African-American spirituals and gospels.[54] This does not mean congregations that are distinctively African American sing only African-American spirituals and gospels. In the African-American church, Caucasian Protestant hymns, especially those of Isaac Watts and the Wesley brothers, are also part of the repertoire, even today. Even though these songs from the Caucasian Protestant tradition are used in the many African-American congregations, they do not always conform to the dictates of the Caucasian Protestant traditions. Many times, they are modified to fit in with the African-American traditions.

Spirituals

"The Spirituals are the heart music of all other American music. They are the taproot of the musical expression of the black religious experience."[55]

The spirituals are a reflection of African background patterns. When Africans were brought to America, they brought with them the art of storytelling through music. Therefore, African-American spirituals reveal African experiences.[56]

Spirituals did not originate in Africa. Spirituals came about as a result of the slave system in America. They told a story of a people who were disenfranchised. They expressed the human emotions of a people who were held captive and treated as less than human. They told the story of the hardship and struggle African Americans had to endure.[57] The theme of the spirituals is freedom from slavery and hope for a better tomorrow. When one listens to the words of the spirituals, he or she is listening to the minds of a people in slavery. They expressed their hopes, fears, thoughts, feelings, and faith in God. The spirituals deal with the life of the slaves in and out of church. They deal with their religious life, as well as their social condition. The spirituals tell the story of how African Americans made an effort to receive freedom here on earth.

In his work, *The Spirituals and the Blues*, James H. Cone points out that W. E. B. DuBois emphasized he saw more in the spirituals than pain and sorrow. DuBois also saw an affirmation of life in the spirituals. Through all of the sorrow of the spirituals, and despite the presence of slavery and oppression, there is faith that there will come a time when men and women will be judged by their souls and not by the color of their skins.[58] In the spirituals, there is the faith that trouble will not last always. Despite the situation slaves were in, shining through the spirituals is a belief that something better is in store.

In her work, *Great American Negroes in Verse*, Eloise Crosby Culver put her thoughts about the spirituals in a poem:

We'd like to tell you all about
The negro and his songs.
They were his bit of Heaven in
A world of many wrongs.

He wrapped himself in melody,
Rode high upon the clouds.
He talked right to his Savior in
The cotton fields and crowds.

His song might send a message while
He slaved throughout the day,
To say, "We will escape tonight,"
While chanting "Steal away!"

When DuBois read the words of the spirituals, he also was fascinated by the tension in them between hope and despair, joy and sorrow, and death and life, and at the ability of the slaves to include both sides of their lives and their experiences in their songs.[60] In the spirituals, the slaves were able to paint a picture of their whole life. The slaves would sing about a better life, but they also were able to sing about the reality of what was happening in their present lives.

The spiritual represents a cultural value which emphasizes free expression and group participation. Spirituals almost always are accompanied by gestures, dance, and verbal interjections. The spiritual is distinguished by the call-and-response structure. The person leading the song, who presents the call, is free to improvise at will, while the congregation provides a stable, repetitive response.[61] The style of the spiritual was established by slave preachers, who improvised songs and added a musical tone to their sermons. This motivated song responses from the congregations. Musical trends were set by those African-American preachers during the times they were unsupervised by slave owners.[62]

"Independent black congregations had the freedom to engage in a form of worship reflecting their own cultural perspectives and musical tradition which emerged out of an African rather than an Euro-American heritage."[63] Although spirituals were created during the time of slavery, they are still a part of worship in some African-American congregations. African Americans still find the songs a source of inspiration and hope.

According to Benjamin Mays, the spirituals provided an emotional security for oppressed slaves during turbulent times. Because they had no security in this world, they put their trust in Jesus, who they believed would make everything all right.[64] Even today, African-American spirituals are still providing some emotional security for those African Americans who feel oppressed because of the troubles of this world.

Black Metered Music

"The term meter is merely borrowed from the music vocabulary to describe a newly shaped folk-form originating with hymns by Isaac Watts, which are referred to as 'Dr. Watts.'"[65] This style of singing in African-American worship, dating from the early 19th century, was influenced by the a cappella "call-and-response" technique used both in spirituals and in the "lining tradition" of early Euro-Americans.[66]

This is done by one person "tuning" one or two lines of a song in a "singsong" fashion. The congregation then "flows in" and sings the same line with some elaboration of the tune. As soon as the first one or two lines are completed, the song leader tunes the next line. It is the leader's task to keep the song going. Sometimes, the last stanza of a song is "moaned," that is, the melody is used without the words. This type of singing is usually performed without the accompaniment of musical instruments. An example of this form of singing follows:

LEADER: I was a wandering sheep

I did not love the fold

CONGREGATION:

I---w-as a wan-der-ing sheep---,

I---di-d not lo-ve- the fo-ld--

LEADER: I would not hear my Shepherd's voice,

I would not be controlled

CONGREGATION:

I--- wou--ld not hear--- my Shepherd's vo--ice

I--- wou--ld n--ot be-- con-- trol--led[67]

African Americans appropriated the hymns of Isaac Watts and others of similar genre and used them for their own religious needs. Worshipers took what was shared with them and made it into something of their own.[68]

Improvised Hymns

The way we sing the hymn today could be described as a song of adoration and praise to God. There was a time when the term *hymn* was applied to all songs in praise of the Lord.[69] Between 1607 and 1790, African Americans often worshiped in churches with Caucasians, and sang the same music. Toward the end of the 18th century, African Americans began to leave these congregations and establish their own places of worship. The format they used in their worship had the same appearance of the format used in the Caucasian churches, but there was a big difference in the music. They took those hymns learned in the Caucasian churches and added their own experiences, which created original African-American hymns.[70]

Even though African Americans were composers and authors of religious songs, they also incorporated Euro-American hymns into their worship.[71] They would take the Euro-American hymns and change the structure of them, because the Euro-American structure did not meet their needs. By changing the structure of the music, African Americans were able to make it their own. They could take Euro-American hymns and sing them with slight variations. African Americans had a way of putting themselves into the songs, and running up and down the scale, in an emotional manner, and remaining in time with the music. They changed the songs to a mode of singing that was common to the African-American religious experience.

Black Gospel

When this writer speaks of Black Gospel, he is well aware African Americans are not the only people who sing gospel music. This writer is cognizant of the fact gospel music is sung in some Caucasian churches, as well. However, there is a distinction in the way the gospel music is sung in the African-American churches. Gospel music in the African-American church has a distinct sound of its own.

The Depression era produced this musical artform known as "gospel." The "gospel" roots are in the African-American religious experience. Gospel music came about during the nation's worst economic crisis.[72]

In the earliest independent African-American church, the music consisted of spirituals and lined-out hymns. The addition of musical instruments to the traditional accompaniment of handclapping and footstomping led to the emergence of an African-American religious music known as gospel.[73]

The term *gospel* was given to this 20th-century style of music by Thomas A. Dorsey, an African-American musician. Melva Wilson Costen said, "In a personal interview, Dorsey indicated gospel music (as opposed to white gospel hymns) is best expounded 'by one who has walked the path of trouble and hard times.'"[74]

Gospel music is religious folk music which can be identified by the social circumstance of the African-American community. Gospel music is an individual expression of a crisis that has been put within a religious context.[75]

The gospel singer is not only expected to sing but is also expected to perform. To get the most out of a gospel song, it is important the singer be seen, as well as heard. The gospel singer is expected to communicate not only through the words of the song but also with the body. The singer uses the hands, feet, and head. A total involvement is demonstrated by the singer.

Summary

To understand that the nature of Christian worship in the African-American church is different from that of the Caucasian church, one must have some knowledge of the history of African-American worship. It must be understood that, unlike the Caucasian church, the African-American church is a product of racism and was founded during the time of slavery. Africans were brought to America against their will and enslaved, but they brought with them the old ways of the African traditional religions. African Americans took the African religions, mixed them with the religion given to them in America, and transformed them into something that met their needs. Because of the social history of African Americans, there were needs that were peculiar to themselves. The only place their needs could be met was in a congregation of people who could identify with the pains and sufferings brought on by slavery and be able to worship God in their own way. This history created a need for a hiding place where African Americans could be free to develop a worship life of their own.

Out of those secret places of worship, a unique African-American faith was developed that assured them there was deliverance from their oppression and hope for the future. It was unique, in that, it was peculiar to the social history of African Americans. This faith gave them strength to hold out and see more in themselves than what they had been told.

The unique faith carried with it some distinctive ways of expressing faith in worship. The songs, prayers, and sermons contained metaphors expressing a life that was different. They expressed hope, faith, and love of a community of people that was different because of its history. The metaphors that were used told of the realities of the present life and, at the same time, celebrated the future life.

Conclusion

Slavery now is over. Progress in the area of race relations has been made in America. Most of those old patterns of racial segregation and discrimination that caused African Americans so much pain no longer exist. There are no longer separate water fountains and separate rest rooms. African Americans no longer have to go to the back door of restaurants and ask for food. There is also the freedom to vote in political elections. African Americans now are able to worship freely without the fear of losing their lives because of some master, but racism is still alive. The same race of people that was excluded because of racism during the time of slavery is still, to some degree, being excluded because of racism even today.

The door of opportunity is opened a little wider now, and some African Americans have managed to get through, but society is still not at the point of declaring that there is equal opportunity for all and being truthful in that declaration. Even those who manage to get through the door of opportunity discover racism is also on the inside. There are still those who make it their business, in some form or fashion, to deliver a message that says, "African Americans are inferior," subsequently, African Americans are treated accordingly. Therefore, those African Americans who meet at the African-American church on Sunday mornings to worship the Lord still are not truly free. They still are dragging the ball and chain of racism. They still are toting the bale of discrimination. They still are carrying the sack of economic segregation. All come, suffering from some state of oppression, but they come to church to worship God because they have hope. They keep going, in spite of the evil forces of life. They refuse to hang their harps upon the willows and stop singing the Lord's song. Therefore, they gather, asking the question, "Is there any word from the Lord?"

They continue to come together because they believe the Lord is able to lift them above the situations of life and give them hope for a better day. They continue to come together because they believe, even in the midst of the prison of life, the Lord is able to set them free. Worship enables African Americans to survive in a world where some people still view them as being inferior. In the midst of the praying, singing, testifying, and preaching, they are able to receive a necessary boost to carry them another day, another week.

African Americans gather on Sunday mornings to give God the praise for bringing them through another week, for giving them the strength to survive another week of racism, abuse, and all the other problems of this world. African-American worship occurs as a result of what God has done, is doing, and will do for all His children. In these worship settings, burdens get lighter, problems get smaller, and hope shines through in the presence of Jesus Christ.

During the time of slavery, one impulse behind African-American worship was the need for a positive self-image. There was the need for a positive self image, dignity, and worth. This positive self-image gave them a purpose and mission in life. It defined for them their true place in the universe.[76]

This is still a major goal of African Americans at times of worship. They still are seeking a positive self-image, healing, wholeness, and a purpose and mission in life. African Americans believe this positive self-image can be found in God, who is the source of their self-worth. During worship, African Americans do not have to worry about being less than some other individual, for they believe that, in God's sight, all are equal. This message of equality is given in many of the songs, prayers, testimonies, sermons, and other aspects of the worship service. When African Americans come together and are able to triumph over personal problems and the problems of the world, there is a feeling of value within the Christian family.

The African-American church is an extended family for African Americans. Therefore, when African Americans gather for worship, they are having a family reunion. At church, they find common ground and a sense of community. This idea of family gives a sense of personal worth and a basis for support. In that family environment, with the help of the Holy Spirit, they are able to experience freedom and a feeling of affirmation. Healing takes place when they discover that the Word of God speaks to their situations and gives them the power needed to transcend the troubles of this world and experience feelings of positive self-worth.

These feelings create a cause for celebration. African-American worship appeals to the emotions as well as the intellect. African Americans rejoice in worship when the Word of God speaks to their condition and when they are able to give God the credit for their being. There is a feeling of thanksgiving for being able to survive another week in a strange land.

These emotions are expressed, in many cases, in what is known as "shouting." Shouting occurs when the worshiper is filled with the Holy Spirit to the point of not being able to keep still. In the words of W. E. B. DuBois,

> When the Spirit of the Lord passed by, and, seizing the devotee, made him mad with supernatural joy, was the last essential of Negro religion and the one more devoutly believed in than all the rest. It varied in expression from the silent rapt countenance or the low murmur and moan to the mad abandon of physical fervor the stamping, shrieking, and shouting, the rushing to and fro and wild waving of arms, the weeping and laughing, the vision and the trance...And so firm a hold did it have on the Negro, that many generations firmly believed that without this visible manifestation of the God there could be no true communion with the invisible.[77]

This experience is a moment of happiness and joy that cannot be programmed into the order of worship but is a response to the presence of God. African Americans become a part of the worship, not just spiritually and mentally, but also vocally and physically. The response may be revealed in a variety of ways. The way in which emotions are expressed depends on the personality of the individual, the worshiper's personal situation at the particular time, along with the preaching, singing, praying, testifying, or the shouting of another worshiper. In expressing themselves from a physical standpoint, worshipers sometimes jump out of their seats and scream and holler, get up and run up and down the aisle, stand and rock from side to side, sit and cry, sit and smile, and just wave their hands. A familiar expression among

African Americans following a Spirit-filled worship experience is, "We had church today." The insinuation is that the Holy Spirit moved in with such power that worshipers were lifted above their problems and concerns and were able to have a good time with the Lord.

CHAPTER 4
Rituals and Ordinances

Preparation for Worship

There are some rituals or acts of preparation for worship that started many years ago in the African-American community. It is believed these rituals began during the times of slavery. There were Saturday night cleansing rituals. African Americans would get their baths on Saturday night for Sunday. They would also lay out the clothes they were going to wear to church and shine their shoes. The African-American worshipers evidently felt it was important to worship God with clean bodies and be as dressed up as possible.[1]

Many families would prepare the Sunday meal on Saturday. This gave those who cooked the freedom to devote Sunday to worship activities, which often lasted well into Sunday evening. These rituals were carried out on Saturday instead because it was believed the Sabbath was to be dedicated to the Lord as a day of rest. Their belief facilitated the shaping of unwritten African-American laws about certain activities to avoid on Sunday. This strengthened the concept of Sunday as a special day for spiritual development.

When there was no preaching at certain churches, sometimes, worshipers would attend Sunday school and then attend a church where there was preaching. The only mode of transportation many African Americans had was walking. Some families would walk miles to attend worship.[2] Some of these rituals continued with some African Americans for many years after slavery ended.

I remember living on a farm in Brownsville, Tennessee, from 1951 to 1962. During these years, my parents kept some of these rituals alive. After working in the fields all week, on Saturday night, the family would take turns with a No. 2 wash tub and the P & G soap taking baths. Clothes that were to be worn to church were checked on Saturday to make sure they were cleaned and ironed. Many African Americans did not have a choice as to what to wear to church, for they had only one outfit suitable for the occasion. Clothes designated as church clothes were usually the best clothes they owned. It was important to African Americans to put on their best when attending church services. Some people called clothes designated for church, "Sunday-go-to-meetin' clothes." The one pair of "Sunday shoes" were also cleaned and polished on Saturday. There would be no ironing of clothes and polishing of shoes on Sunday because that was the Lord's day.

I lived about 2 miles from church, and the mode of transportation was walking unless it was raining. If it was raining at the time we were to leave for church, the mode of transportation would be mules and a wagon.

Children were very careful about the games they played on Sunday evenings; after church, some games were forbidden. There definitely would be no playing ball, for it was considered a sin to play ball on Sunday. No work was done on Sundays except that which was considered absolutely necessary, such as feeding and watering the livestock and bringing in wood for fires which usually was cut on Saturday.

Even today, there are those who lay out their Sunday clothes and shine their shoes on Saturday in preparation for Sunday worship, and many African Americans attend Sunday morning worship wearing the best they have. It is still believed by many African Americans that they should appear before the Lord clean and well dressed. There was a request from a couple of young adult members of the congregation of which I am pastor that the church have dress down or "come-as-you-are" days. An older member of the

70

congregation said, "Pastor, I do not agree with that, for, if we dress down, we will act down, and there should be no acting down in God's house. We act better when we dress up for God, and this should be taught to our young people. We should wear our best when coming to church."

Conversion

During the time of slavery, slaves did not have the opportunity to adapt to the world around them. The only world from which the slaves could develop a scale of values to judge the world around them and themselves was an inner world. The masters did not understand the spiritual cravings of the slaves. No respect was ever paid to the right of their emotions for any outlet. Most Caucasians denied that African Americans had any kind of emotions except primitive emotions. Very little effort was made to bring the slaves into contact with the form of Christianity prevailing in the antebellum South. For, what value could Christianity have for a people whose holiest feelings were being daily and cold-heartedly disregarded? This misinterpretation was bound to leave the victims with a sense of degradation.[3]

The slaves' prayers for deliverance from their sins went beyond the things they did that were considered sins. What they wanted was cleansing and a rebirth.[4] They were not concerned about what they did to get themselves into a sinful condition. Their primary concern was to be made new, to have a close relationship with their God. The conversion experiences have changed the lives of generations of African Americans since the days of slavery. To African Americans, conversion represented more than just a change in behavior. It represented a change of heart, a transformation in consciousness, and a reorientation of personality.[5]

For African Americans, the conversion experience was an experience that changed the whole person. There was expected to be a change in behavior, but it was because of the change that occurred on the inside as a result of the conversion experience. They saw themselves as being new individuals. They believed old had passed away and all things had become new.

Africans and their descendants in Protestant America discovered beliefs and rituals in the revivals similar to those of Africa. This was very crucial to the African Americans because these practices helped them better understand and adapt to Christianity. In Africa, there were rituals of initiation in many societies, including induction into adulthood. Some of the symbols used incorporated death and rebirth, which were consistent with the symbols of Christian conversion. In the revivals, they witnessed such outward expressions as shouting, clapping, and drumming, reminding them of the presence of the divine in many African religions.[6]

The conversion experience of the African Americans was more than just a personal action, for it also was defined and validated within the congregation. The influence of preachers, other church leaders, and parents on the conversion experience gave it magnitude. This guidance and validation were built into the process of conversion. This was something that began in adolescence. Conversion was a social method for the initiation of adolescents into the community for generations of African Americans. African-American children were expected to experience conversion.[7]

Although conversion is a personal experience for the African American, it is not individualistic, because both the person's immediate family and the church family have great influence over the entire conversion process. It is personal, yet also communal. Christian parents start preparing their children for conversion at an early age by teaching them and getting them involved in church activities, especially Sunday church school. When the children finally experience conversion, the community feels proud and relieved. The members are proud because so many people feel they were in some way instrumental in causing this to happen; they are relieved because the devil has missed a soul he thought he had, and the soul is bound for heaven.

Emphasizing the community involvement in the conversion in no way negates the power of the personal side of the experience. The conversion experience for the enslaved was a deep, personal experience because it had an impact on their entire lives. In the words of Raboteau,

> The resonances of this sacred drama upon the daily conditions of the rest of their lives should not be underestimated. When the narrators spoke of their conversion as a rebirth, of being made entirely new, of being filled with love for everything and everybody, they revealed the depth of internal transformation that defined their identity and self worth. For those facing the dehumanizing conditions of enslavement, the daily physical, psychological, and emotional attacks against one's dignity as a person, to experience the total acceptance and affirmation of self by God challenged the mentality of slavery at a fundamental level.[8]

Another conversion tradition was the "mourners' bench." The mourners' bench was usually the front pew in the church. If there was a center row of pews, it was the front pew of the center row. Mourners were those individuals who were not Christians but who had the desire to become Christians. The preacher usually would ask if such people were in the worship service and invite them to come sit on the "mourners' bench." While they were sitting there, other members would pray for their conversion. In some cases, the preacher would ask the mourners to get up and go find someone in the congregation to pray for them. Each chosen person would go to the mourners' bench with the mourner and kneel behind him or her and pray. In the prayer, a plea was made to God to save this sinner and make him or her a part of the Christian family.

Those who received salvation as a result of going to the mourners' bench demonstrated to the congregation that God had brought them through. It was believed the person must undergo some emotionally transforming experience. The believer was expected to come off of the mourners' bench in some emotional manner, indicating to the members of the congregation that salvation had taken place. It was believed that, in order to receive salvation, the believer must feel the presence of the Holy Spirit. The believer was expected to get up either crying or shouting to demonstrate to those in the congregation that God had moved in his or her life. The believer was saying, "Yes, I feel something; I have religion; I am changed." The act usually occurred during revival week.

Albert B. Cleage, Jr., in his work, *Black Christian Nationalism: New Directions for the Black Church*, asserts,

> The process of being saved was built around the old mourners' bench. Sinners were convicted of their sins by preaching and came forward to be saved. Coming down front indicated only a desire to be saved. The process of being saved was a group experience participated in by everyone present. The congregation would pray, sing, shout, and scream until the walls of individualism crumbled and the sinner confessed and became a part of the group. At that moment he had a conscious experience of God and he was saved. The old mourners' bench represented a process by which an individual submerged himself in a group and escaped from individualism.[9]

Of course, the mourners' bench is not as prevalent now as in previous years. It is now considered by some to be old-fashioned. It is believed by some to be embarrassing to ask publicly if people are sinners and separate them from the Christians by putting them on a special pew.

Baptism and the Lord's Supper

Baptism and the Lord's Supper have been considered central among the many acts and expressions of public worship since New Testament times.[10] "Early Christian worship combined both the inward attitude and the outward symbols representing the gospel as revealed in Jesus Christ."[11] In his writings, the apostle Paul emphasized spiritual and symbolic acts. He said, "For by one Spirit are we all baptized into one body...and have been all made to drink into one Spirit" (1 Cor. 12.13, KJV). The whole body of Christianity shares in the blood and body of Christ. Paul also said, "For we being many are one bread, and one body: for we are all partakers of that one bread" (1 Cor. 10:17, KJV). Baptism and the Lord's Supper are represented by outward symbols, which convey the truth of the Gospel. When they are performed as acts of worship, they witness to the Gospel and God's grace.[12]

The symbols of water, bread, and wine are deeply significant for Christian worship. The reason these particular symbols and actions are important in Christian worship is because we did not choose them. They were chosen for us in the context of the acts of God in history. They point to the redemptive actions of God in the life, death, and resurrection of Jesus Christ.[13]

Baptism

The symbol used in the act of baptism is water. Baptism, for Baptists, is defined as the immersion in water of a believer in Christ, into the name of the Father, Son, and Holy Ghost. It is an act of obedience, which symbolizes the faith of the believer in a crucified, buried, and risen Savior. It also symbolizes the believers' death to sin, the burial of the old life, and the resurrection to walk in newness of life in Christ Jesus. Baptists believe that, in order to become a member of the church and partake of the Lord's Supper, one must first be baptized by immersion. Baptists believe baptism is an external symbol of the internal salvation and that no external physical act can produce salvation.

"At the heart of the doctrine is 'believers' baptism' by immersion."[14] Baptists believe salvation must be experienced before baptism has any meaning. The act of baptism by immersion in water is a symbol of a spiritual act which takes place in the soul of the one who has responded in faith to the Gospel by accepting Jesus Christ as Savior and Lord.

Water is the element most naturally used for the cleansing of the body. When water is used in the act of baptism, it is a symbol of cleansing from the old way of living and the beginning of a new life. Those who accept Christ as Savior and Lord and receive baptism by water experience the cleansing of the Holy Spirit.

Slaves and Baptism

Baptisms apparently lifted the spirits of slaves and caused excitement in the slave communities. The news about a baptismal service traveled fast throughout the slave communities. Slaves and free men and women were known to have walked several miles to attend a baptism and share in the excitement of the occasion. From an African perspective, when one moved from one stage in life to another, it was a time of celebration. People wanted to be witnesses to the change that takes place in rituals of death and regeneration.[15]

The candidates would dress in white, and those who already had been baptized would escort the candidates to the pond or creek to be baptized. The congregation would be standing near, where they could watch the preacher dunk the candidates in the waters of death and resurrection. They would sometimes come out of the water shouting "Hallelujah."[16]

Baptism in ponds or other bodies of water did not stop after slavery. When I was about 9 or 10 years old, I went to Memphis, Tennessee, to spend a weekend with my older brother. On that Sunday afternoon, the family went to a lake somewhere in Mississippi, where a baptism of this nature took place. I watched the preacher make his way out into the lake until the water reached his waist. The congregation was standing on the bank of the lake, singing songs and praying. One by one, the candidates for baptism were escorted out in the water to the preacher, where he said the appropriate words and dunked them under the water. When they came up out of the water, the people rejoiced.

Most churches today have indoor baptisteries; therefore, people are not being baptized in open bodies of water like they once were, but the process and the meaning of baptism are the same. At the church of which I am pastor, a baptismal service is held on a first Sunday of the month, immediately after Sunday school and right before morning worship. On many occasions, people travel for miles just to witness the baptism of a relative or friend and be a part of the celebration.

The Lord's Supper

Another meaningful act of worship is the Lord's Supper. The Lord's Supper is one of the ordinances which Jesus gave to His church. The Lord's Supper is commemorative of the death and sufferings of Jesus Christ. The original elements used in this ordinance were bread and wine. Although today, instead of wine, many churches use grape juice. The bread symbolizes the body of Christ given for the salvation of mankind, and the wine, symbolizes His blood shed for the remission of sins. The Lord's Supper is an outward sign referring to the relationship between Jesus and Christians. When worshipers partake of the elements, they are participating in the death of Jesus for the sins of the world.

The Lord's Supper is really a memorial service, Paul said, "For as often as you eat this bread and drink the cup, you proclaim the Lord's death until he comes" (1 Cor. 11:26, NRSV). The Supper represents the continuing presence of the crucified, risen Savior to remind His people of what He promised. When He said, "'This is my body…this is my blood,'" (Matt. 14:22-24, NIV), He implied that the observance with bread and wine always would be a reminder that He is present with His people at worship.

Slaves and the Lord's Supper

There is very little documentation of slave involvement in the celebration of the Lord's Supper, although it is believed that slaves who had been baptized and received into the fellowship of any Protestant church could participate in the Lord's Supper.[17]

In order to participate in the Lord's Supper, one had to pass a test. During the week prior to the celebration of the Lord's Supper, a service of preparation was held. Those people desiring the privilege of participating in the Lord's Supper would be asked questions concerning their piety and Christian discipline. Their answers would determine whether they would receive a token that would serve as a pass to the celebration of the Lord's Supper. The tokens for African Americans differed from the tokens of Euro-Americans. The African Americans' tokens were pewter, and the tokens for the Euro-Americans were silver.[18] A person who had lived a sinful life was not allowed to be a part of this celebration. Only those who let their lights shine as Christians during the week were worthy to partake of the elements representing the body and blood of Jesus Christ.

When the African Americans celebrated the Lord's Supper with Caucasians, it came after the preaching. The Caucasians would come to the table and be served first. Those African Americans with tokens would be served last. They would come down from the balcony or from some other reserved seating, present their tokens, and receive the bread and wine.[19]

Even though there were times when African Americans were excluded from the Lord's Supper by the early evangelists, African Americans still believe in it and celebrate it. Jesus' eating, drinking, and fellowshipping with common folk must have strengthened the importance of the Lord's Supper for African Americans. One who is concerned for the hungry, invites the poor to dinner, and welcomes tax collectors and sinners to eat with Him surely would share a meal with social outcasts of any age and culture.

CHAPTER 5
Elements of a Sample Worship

It is my belief that the order of worship should be in a form that will cause the congregation to become involved in a meaningful worship experience. The worship service should be structured in a manner that meets the needs of the whole congregation. This requires much prayer and planning on the part of the worship leader.

The Bible says, "God is a Spirit; and they that worship him must worship him in spirit and in truth" (John 4:24, KJV). The "truth" is the content, which is God's Word. In His great, high priestly prayer, Jesus invoked the Father on our behalf, and He prayed, "Sanctify them through thy truth: thy word is truth" (John 17:17). This "truth" must be put in the form or order of worship. Each of the elements in the order of worship should reflect the Scripture readings and the sermon, so the congregation might be led to a well-rounded worship experience.

Although the worship service should have a meaningful form, it also should have spontaneity. "No act of worship can be acceptable to God unless it be spontaneous and sincere."[1] The worship should not be cut-and-dried but should allow freedom of the Holy Spirit. There should be order, but the order also should be flexible enough to allow the Spirit to be in control. A congregation never should become a slave to the order, but should allow its freedom to make use of the order. The order of worship varies as to its content among African-American churches. The order in which the elements are listed also deviates.

However, the following is an example of an order of worship in an African-American church:

THE DEVOTION . . . . .Praise Team or Deacons in Charge

THE PRELUDE . . . . .Musicians

THE CALL TO WORSHIP

PASTOR   Praise ye the Lord; Praise God in his sanctuary;
                      Praise him in the firmament of power.

CONGREGATION   Praise him for his mighty acts;
                      Praise him according to his excellent greatness.

TOGETHER   Let every thing that hath breath praise the Lord.
                      Praise ye the Lord.

THE PROCESSIONAL

THE INVOCATION . . . . .Pastor

THE PRAYER RESPONSE . . . . .Choir

THE RESPONSIVE READING

THE GLORIA PATRI . . . . .Glory Be to the Father

THE HYMN OF PRAISE . . . . .Choir and Congregation

THE OFFERING FOR MISSIONS

THE READING OF GOD'S WORD . . . . .Pastor

THE MORNING PRAYER . . . . .Deacon

THE CONGREGATIONAL HYMN . .Choir and Congregation

THE ANNOUNCEMENTS

THE WELCOME TO VISITORS

THE PASTORAL OBSERVATIONS . . . . .Pastor

THE CHILDREN'S TIME

THE SELECTION . . . . .Choir

THE OFFERTORY:

                      The Offertory Sentences
                      The Tendering of God's Tithes
                      The Giving of Our Offering
                      The Presentation of the Gifts
                      The Prayer of Thanksgiving
                      The Offertory Response

THE SELECTION . . . . .Choir

THE PRAYER AND MEDITATION . . . . .Pastor

THE SPOKEN WORD .... Pastor

THE CALL TO CHRISTIAN DISCIPLESHIP .... Pastor

THE INVITATIONAL SELECTION .... Choir

THE ALTAR CALL

THE CLOSING SONG .... Choir

THE BENEDICTION .... Pastor

THE POSTLUDE .... Musicians

The Devotion

The devotion is the element in the order of worship in the African-American Baptist church in which the worshipers are given a chance to express themselves. The devotion is an informal service where, normally, the deacons lead the congregation in songs, prayers, and testimonies. The worshipers are given an opportunity to testify—to tell of the good things God has done for them—to lift up the name of Jesus, as an individual and as a community.

According to James Cone, the testimony is an integral part of the African-American religious tradition. It is the occasion in which a believer stands before the congregation and gives an account of the hope they have. The testimony, in an African-American worship experience, is the believers' personal stories of how God has taken care of them in the midst of trials. The purpose of testimony is to strengthen the faith of those hearing the testimony and also to build the faith of the community.[2] The testimony gives hope to the listeners that God can do the same things for them which have been done and are being done for the one giving the testimony. Cone also said, "There may be persons who are discouraged and do not know whether they can overcome the 'principalities and powers' of the world. The testimony of a fellow believer reminds them that 'though the way may be dark and the road rocky,' I am a living witness that the Lord will make a way somehow."[3] Testimonies provide an opportunity for those committed believers to help be a witness to what God can and will do in the life of a Christian.

Individuals are strengthened by listening to each other's testimonies and joining in with them in singing, praying, and witnessing for the Lord. Some worshipers enjoy this element of worship because it is informal and lay people are usually in charge. The deacons are there to keep it structured and in order. The devotion is a preparation period.

Increasingly, African-American churches are organizing praise teams. Praise teams are taking the place of the traditional devotion with the deacons leading the congregation in prayers and testimonies. Praise teams lead the congregation in singing praise songs. The goal is the same as with the deacons in charge. Both are present to get the congregation actively involved in the worship experience.

The devotion should prepare the worshipers' hearts and minds for worshiping and receiving the Word of God. In the African-American church, the devotion is referred to as the time to get things "heated up" for the expected message from the preacher.

The Prelude

The organ prelude signals the end of the devotional period. It creates an atmosphere and provides an introduction to the remainder of the worship service. The organ music prior to the beginning of the worship is intended to get the people's attention and prepare them to meet God in worship.

The Call to Worship

The call to worship consists of "Scriptural sentences or words proclaiming God in Jesus the Christ has taken the initiative to call the people to worship."[4]

The Processional

The processional is an opening hymn, or other appropriate song, sung by the choir while the group is making its way to the choir loft. The processional should not be a song focusing on human needs or conditions but of praise to God. A worship service always should be structured in a manner where in God will be acknowledged and praised before human wants or needs are mentioned.

The Invocation

The first formal prayer in the order of worship at the Zion Memorial Baptist Church is called the invocation. The invocation is the opening prayer, in which adoration and praise are the main elements. The purpose of the invocation is to lead the people to become conscious of God's presence and to open their hearts to receive His blessings.

The Prayer Response

At the end of the invocation, there is a prayer response, like an "Amen" to the prayer. This response is sung by the choir at the end of the prayer. Normally, the person praying the prayer of invocation does not say "Amen" at the end of the prayer but waits until after the singing of the response and says "Amen" with the choir. The prayer response is a way of expressing approval of and agreeing with what has just been said in the invocation.

The Responsive Reading

There are different ways of reading the Scriptures in worship. The Scripture may be read responsively, with the pastor or a lay person reading a verse or phrase of Scripture, then the congregation reading a verse or phrase, and so on. The responsive reading encourages participation of the worshipers.

The Gloria Patri

The Gloria Patri is a song of praise to God.

The Hymns

One type of music that is present in the worship at the Zion Memorial Baptist Church is the hymn. For many African Americans, using a hymnal is almost like using a Bible. Some worshipers will look for hymns with words fitting their present situation, and they put themselves in the seat of the hymnologist. The singing of some hymns has a way of strengthening worshipers and giving them the necessary courage to hold on in the midst of their situations.

The singing of the hymns also gives the congregation an opportunity to be a part of the worship. Congregational singing is important because it is a way of bringing worshipers together and giving them a feeling of unity. I am of the belief that there should be an opportunity for all worshipers to sing together, and they should be encouraged to do so. Congregational singing gives all members an opportunity to express their innermost thoughts.

The Reading of God's Word

"The reading of the Bible is in itself an act of worship— not the worship of the written Word but the worship of the living Word to whom the written Word gives witness."[5] I believe the Word of God to be central in worship. Without the Word of God, there can be no worship. God reveals Himself to humanity through His words. The Bible is a record of the acts of God in history as revealed to humanity by the Holy Spirit.

The reading of Scripture was an element in early Christian worship. We are told Jesus stood up in the synagogue to read the Scripture (Luke 4:16). Paul makes several references to the reading of the Scripture (Col. 4:16; 1 Thess. 5:27; 1 Tim. 4:13). Paul's letters were written to be read in the churches to which they were addressed.

The Bible is the life book of the church. It is a book of guidance, which helps people gain more knowledge about

God's will. The Bible is the book of authority for Christian life. When the Bible is read, it honors God and brings comfort and peace to the worshipers.

The Morning Prayer

The next formal prayer in the order of service at Zion Memorial Baptist Church is called the "morning prayer." This prayer is prayed by a deacon or some other lay member. This gives an opportunity to those other than the pastor to approach God in prayer and express their innermost feelings to Him.

The person praying this prayer usually prays not only for himself/herself but for the welfare of the entire congregation. There are concerns for those present in the congregation. Intercession for those who are absent from the fellowship; for the community; for local, state, and national leaders, and other concerns of the congregation are sometimes mentioned to God in this prayer. The person praying will usually pray also for the sick and shut-in of the church. Some people will even call individuals' names in their prayers. There is one person in my church who, when he prays the morning prayer, prays not only for individuals and calls them by name, but also prays for individual auxiliaries and boards and calls them by name.

Prayers prayed aloud in African-American worship strengthen those who are listening and praying along silently with the person leading. They will sometimes respond with their "Amens."

The Announcements

The announcements are very important and necessary in the African-American congregation. In the words of Dearing E. King,

> This is necessary because the black church through its spiritual creativity gave birth to many black organizations, businesses, and movements. Therefore, time has to be allowed to promote

the work of such agencies as the NAACP, the Urban League, the Southern Christian Leadership Conference, black newspapers, and so forth. These agencies have fought for black causes when the white church and the federal government failed to do so.[6]

The announcements inform worshipers about what is happening in the community, in the lives of other people, and in the lives of church members. These notifications are a way of keeping the people informed about important events and issues.

The Welcome to Visitors

It is the belief of this writer that the welcome to visitors on behalf of the congregation is in order. The purpose for welcoming visitors at the church where I am pastor is to show humility and appreciation for their choosing this particular church as their place of worship. The welcome to visitors is also a means of encouraging the visitors, early in the service, to participate fully as a part of the extended family.

The welcome, if done properly, can cause visitors to feel at ease and relaxed. When this happens, visitors will be able to worship more freely.

The Pastoral Observations

The pastoral observations are used to inform, enlighten, and inspire. Sometimes, things the worshipers are already aware of are presented from a pastoral point of view. The worshipers may be informed about political or community affairs. Pastoral observations are kept brief so as not to interfere with the spirit of the worship service.

The Children's Time

The children's time is the point in the order of worship where all children are called to the front of the sanctuary and an age-appropriate message designed for them is given. The children's message gives small bits of truths in a short message the children are able to comprehend. This is one way of making the children aware that they are a part of the fellowship of the congregation. It is also a means of training children to participate in the worship service.

The Choir Songs

In the African-American church, choirs play an important role in the worship service. The choirs are responsible for the organized singing of gospel songs, spirituals, anthems, and, sometimes, improvised hymns. A trained choir is a great asset in leading the congregation in worship. The choir has special skills and gifts not necessarily given to the congregation. The choir sharpens and polishes the songs of the congregation. Because the choir members sharpen their skills by rehearsing on a regular basis, they are able to offer what the congregation cannot offer. The choir selections can be an inspiration to the congregation and really help the worship service if the music is appropriate for the occasion.

The Tithes and Offering

The giving of material possessions is not always done freely in worship. It has been my experience that this attitude is present in some worshipers because of a lack of teaching at a young age. It seems as though the older some people get, the more they get set in their ways and do not want to change. It is much easier to get young adults to give freely of their tithes and offerings than the middle aged and older. People must be taught at an early age the significance of giving of their tithes and offerings in worship. The reason for giving of tithes and offerings in worship goes beyond paying salaries, utilities, benevolence, missions, etc. There is a sound theological basis for offering gifts as an act of worship to God.

In the Old Testament, sacrifice was the essential act of external worship. In the very act of sacrifice, a personal union with God was achieved, for God accepted the offering and also the worshiper who made the sacrifice. Paul refers to this act of sacrifice: "Are not they which eat the sacrifices partakers of the altar?" (1 Cor. 10:18b, KJV).

The giving of our gifts is a symbolic act representing the giving of the self. Paul commended the Christians in the churches of Macedonia for their generosity. The real value of their giving is verified by the fact they "first gave their own selves to the Lord" (2 Cor. 8:5, KJV), and their sacrificial giving confirmed their sincerity.

When people give just to keep the doors of the church open or just because the pastor or someone else encourages them to give, they may miss the blessing of giving. When people realize that everything belongs to God and that they are only managers of God's gifts, and if they share what they have out of gratitude for what God has entrusted to them, they may never get tired of giving. Giving with the belief that God owns everything and human beings are only managers of God's gifts makes people see the offering as an opportunity to care, share, and participate in the wholeness of life.

When we worship through the act of giving, we are giving proof of our gratitude to God for His gifts, especially the gift of grace in Christ. Paul's appeal to the Corinthian Christians to share their material goods with the needy people of Macedonia concludes by saying, "Thanks be unto God for his unspeakable gift" (2 Cor. 9:15, KJV).

The Offertory Prayer

The purpose of the offertory prayer is dedication of gifts and self. The prayer usually includes statements of thanksgiving and the use of the gifts. This prayer consists of those matters pertaining only to the tithes and the offerings.

The Offertory Response

The offertory response is sung when the tithes and offerings are presented at the altar. The response serves as a symbol of communion between God and the worshipers.

The Spoken Word

Preaching is an element of worship, not something added to worship, nor something taking place when the worship part of the service is finished. The preaching of the Word of God is the center of worship.

Preaching the Gospel is the business of the church. The preacher's voice is a representative voice of the entire church. The preacher speaks for the church and not merely to the church. With the church, the preacher speaks to the world.[7]

Preaching is proclaiming the Gospel, the Good News of Jesus. Gospel means "Good News;" Good News from God about God, creation, life, the world, and redemption. New Testament preaching is informing humanity of this Good News.

The morning message should confront the congregation with the Word of God to tell them what God did in the days of Jesus, to pass on to them the historical facts recorded in those ancient documents, and to try to persuade them to accept those facts and live by them. This Good News from God can come to the attention of people only if they are told about it. Telling it is preaching.

The message should convince and persuade people to come to decisions and to make commitments. Preaching is done with the hope of bearing fruit, transforming the lives of people, and serving their spiritual needs. Preaching challenges people, uplifts them, comforts and assures them, and sometimes disturbs them with the hope of making them better people. Preaching calls for people to make commitments by responding to the Word of God.

The Call to Christian Discipleship

The call to Christian discipleship gives people an opportunity to come and join the church. This should be a serious time in worship.

The Invitational Song

The invitational selection goes along with the call to Christian discipleship. This is really another way of extending the invitation. It is sung at this point for the purpose of receiving new members into the church. The song should be appropriate for the occasion and should reflect the message of the sermon.

The Altar-Call Prayer

The altar-call prayer in the worship service is prayed when the worshipers are invited to come to the front of the sanctuary for the purpose of praying together. The pastor and congregation unite in hearts and minds as they engage in prayer together. It is a time when the minister becomes the congregation's voice and offers its prayers to God. The altar-call prayer is a prayer when God is given thanks for all His blessings; confessions are made for sins committed; needs of individuals and the entire congregation are presented to God; and Christians are given encouragement and hope.

The Closing Song

The closing song is sung in anticipation of the benediction. The focus of this song is the unity of the worshipers as they prepare to go out to serve.

The Benediction

The last formal prayer in the order of worship at the Zion Memorial Baptist Church is the benediction, unless the Lord's Supper is being served on a given Sunday. The benediction commends the worshipers to God's care and pronounces His blessings on them. The benediction should continue an expression of worship and be offered to God as a commitment of the congregation to go forth into the world to serve.[8]

The Postlude

The postlude sets a good atmosphere for departure. The purpose of the postlude is to carry the worshipers out in an inspirational mood.

CHAPTER 6

Summary

Some Significant Points and Insights

Africans were taken from their native land brought to America, and held in bondage for 200 years. The destiny of many things occurring in the life of the African-American community was determined by the slave owners.

The Baptist church became attractive to slaves because the preaching at the revival services offered them a vision of God's justice. The Baptist invitation came at a time when African Americans were uncomfortable enough with the life they were forced to live to hunger for a better one.

There were scattered instances of African Americans holding membership in Caucasian churches. Although a few African Americans were received as members, they did not have the same freedoms as Caucasians. African Americans were not allowed to participate in the Christian fellowship on an equal basis. For the majority of the already-existing Baptist community, equality meant the loss of power because they believed slavery was the most effective means of social control.

Slavery created spiritual stress and social tensions leading to a separate church movement among African-American Baptists. This occurred because of the way African Americans were treated by Caucasians.

In this book, it is understood that African-American worship is not exclusively applicable to a particular group or race, nor is African-American worship better or worse than any other form of worship. However, the text is an attempt to deal with the reality of differences between African-American churches and primarily Caucasian churches. On Sunday mornings, many African Americans look for churches whose parishioners are predominantly African American and many Caucasians look for churches whose parishioners are predominantly Caucasian.

Because there are different styles of worship in the African-American church, all African-American congregations do not look and sound the same on Sunday morning at worship. The style of worship varies from church to church, and diverse determinant factors are responsible for these variations. Different situations, circumstances, and exposure to Christianity shaped each congregation. Therefore, history, theological orientation, geography, and social lifestyles are significant determinants of worship based on different circumstances.

Although there is a difference in the style of worship, there are also distinctive discernable patterns. To understand that the nature of Christian worship in the African-American church is different from the Caucasian church, one must have some knowledge of the history of African-American worship. This uniqueness stems from the influence of African history and culture on African Americans. African Americans share a common history reaching back to the African soil. African Americans were brought from Africa against their will, enslaved, and treated as less than human by those who were responsible for bringing them to America. This history created a need for communities of refuge and hiding places conducive to authentic communication with God and one another.

There is a vast difference in the histories of African Americans and Caucasians. Unlike the Caucasian church, the African-American church is a product of oppressive racism and was founded during the period of slavery. African Americans were the "oppressed," while Caucasians were the "oppressors." The African-American church was created out of an environment that was totally different from that of the Caucasian church. African Americans were not free to express themselves in worship.

African-American worship was determined on the basis of how African Americans saw and responded to God. This made and makes it a theological matter. Therefore, when we speak of the differences in worship of the African-American church compared to the Caucasian church, we are really pointing to a disparity in the perception of, and response to, God in history, the present moment, and what He promises for the future.

Generally, when African-American congregations gather for worship, informed by their social history, they see God as the One who has been with them in the midst of a racist society and brought them to the present moment. Their perceptions of God, in history and the present, give them the courage to lean on His promises for the future. Therefore, the religion of African Americans is really a theology of hope. They have hope for the future, based on what God has done in the past and is doing in the present. This is not to say that Caucasian congregations do not have hope in God, but Caucasians, in general, they do not come to the same point in their theological interpretation of the acts of God because of the vast differences in their history.

When Africans were brought to America, they carried their religion with them. After a time, they accepted the "white man's" religion, but they have not always expressed it in the "white man's" way. Because of African-American social history, African Americans had needs peculiar to themselves. Because their needs were different, they needed a religion and worship that was different. Therefore, they accepted the existing religion but changed it into a form with which they could identify.

There were times when the slaves actually risked their lives in an effort to develop a worship life of their own. In an effort to find freedom, to understand the biblical message, and to express their own beliefs in response to almighty God, slaves had to find secret places, in which to worship. In these secret places the slaves were able to transform the Christianity that was given them in America into a Christianity that met their needs. As a result, a unique form of African-American faith was developed.

The unique faith carried with it some distinctive ways of expressing faith in worship. The songs, prayers, and sermons contained metaphors expressing a different life. They expressed hope, faith, and love of a community of people that was different because of its history of social oppression. The metaphors used told of the realities of that present life and, at the same time, celebrated the future life.

Worship in the African-American experience is the visible expression of what African Americans believe about God, based on their history. It is a worship experience that includes a black theology. The worship of the African-American church and its life cannot be separated. The expressions in worship are the result of what has happened and is happening in their cooperate life. Therefore, these expressions are unique to African Americans.

I nurture a belief that the African-American Baptist church will continue to be the place where one can go to find community, togetherness, a family environment, and a place where everyone can experience the enriching and necessary bond for himself/herself. I also believe the African-American Baptist church will continue to be an energetic force in the advancement of the Christian faith.

NOTES

Introduction

1. Melva Wilson Costen, *African American Christian Worship* (Nashville: Abingdon Press, 1993), 15-16.

2. Thomas Hoyt, Jr., "The African American Worship Experience and The Bible," *The Journal of the Interdenominational Theological Center* 14 (Fall 1986/Spring 1987): 4-5.

Chapter 1

1. James Melvin Washington, *Frustrated Fellowship: The Black Baptist Quest for Social Power* (Macon: Mercer University Press, 1963), 4.
2. John E. Skoglund, *The Baptists* (Valley Forge: Judson Press, 1967), 10-12.
3. Nancy Tatam Ammerman, *Baptists Battles: Social Change and Religious Conflict in the Southern Baptist Convention* (New Brunswick: Rutgers University Press, 1950), 22.
4. Robert G. Torbet, *A History of the Baptists* (Valley Forge: Judson Press, 1963), 202.
5. Ibid., 203.
6. Skoglund, 22.
7. Robert L. Ferm, "Great Awakening," in *The World Book Encyclopedia*, 1974 ed.
8. Skoglund, 22.
9. William Henry Brackney, *The Baptists* (New York: Greenwood Press, 1988), 87.
10. Torbet, 234.
11. Ibid., 243.
12. Ibid.
13. Ibid., 31.
14. Brackney, 101.

15. Ibid., 101.
16. Ibid., 102.
17. Ibid., 102.
18. Ibid., 17.
19. Ibid., 103.
20. Ibid., 18-19.
21. Ibid., 21.

Chapter 2

1. James H. Cone, *God of the Oppressed* (New York: Seabury Press, 1975), 2.
2. John Hope Franklin, "George Washington Williams and Africa," in Africa and the Afro-American Experience, ed. Lorraine A. Williams (Washington: Howard University Press, 1977), 59.
3. Gayraud S. Wilmore, *Black Religion and Black Radicalism: An Interpretation of the Religious History of Afro-American People* (Maryknoll, New York: Orbis Books, 1983), 100.
4. Kenneth Aran. et al., *The History of Black Americans* (New York: United Federation of Teachers, 1972), 13.
5. Harold A. Carter, Wyatt Tee Walker, William A. Jones, Jr., *The African American Church* (New York: Martin Luther King Fellows Press, 1991), 5.
6. Lerone Bennett, Jr., *Before the Mayflower: A History of the Negro in America* (Chicago: Johnson Publishing Company, Inc., 1966), 70-71.
7. Ibid., 71.
8. Ibid., 82.
9. Benjamin Quarles, *The Negro in the Making of America* (London: Collier-Macmillan LTD, 1964), 67.
10. Ibid., 74.
11. Walter F. Pitts, *Old Ship of Zion: The Afro-Baptist Ritual in the African Diaspora* (New York: Oxford University Press, 1993), 35-36.
12. Ibid., 36-37.
13. John Hope Franklin and Alfred A. Moss, Jr., *From Slavery*

to Freedom: A History of Negro Americans (New York: Alfred A. Knopf Inc., 1947), 119.

14. Pitts, 37.
15. Mechal Sobel, *Trablin' On: The Slave Journey to an Afro-Baptist Faith* (Westport: Greenwood Press, 1979), 99.
16. James Melvin Washington, *Frustrated Fellowship: The Black Baptist Quest for Social Power* (Macon: Mercer University Press, 1963), 7.
17. Sobel, 101.
18. Ibid., 102.
19. Leroy Fitts, *A History of Black Baptists* (Nashville: Broadman Press, 1985), 24-25.
20. W. D. Weatherford, *American Churches and the Negro: An Historical Study from Early Slave Days to the Present* (Boston: Christopher Publishing House, 1957), 119.
21. Albert J. Raboteau, *Slave Religion: The "Invisible Institution" in the Antebellum South* (Oxford: New York: University Press, 1978), 179.
22. Ibid., 180.
23. Fitts, 44.
24. Washington, 16.
25. Ibid., 18.
26. Fitts, 44.
27. Ibid., 43.
28. Washington, 23.
29. William Henry Brackney, *The Baptists* (New York: Greenwood Press, 1988), 18-19.
30. Washington, 23.
31. Ibid., 23.
32. Fitts, 66-67.
33. Brackney, 19.
34. Fitts, 79-106.
35. W. E. B. DuBois, *The Souls of Black Folk* (Chicago: McClurg, 1903; repr., New York: New American Library, 1969), 45-46.
36. James H. Evans, Jr., *We Have Been Believers: An African-American Systematic Theology* (Minneapolis: Fortress

Press, 1992), 112.
37. Alton B. Pollard, III, "Race, Religion, and Resistance in the African American Experience," Speech delivered at the Associacao Nacional Casa Dandara International Seminar, Minas-Centro/Belo Horizonte, Minas Gerais Brazil, 5-10 November 1995.
38. John S. Mbiti, *African Religions and Philosophy* (Garden City, NY: Anchor Books, 1970), 141.

Chapter 3

1. Melva Wilson Costen, *African American Christian Worship* (Nashville: Abingdon Press, 1993), 13-14.
2. Wyatt Tee Walker, *The Soul of Black Worship* (New York: Martin Luther King Fellows Press, 1984), 1.
3. John E. Brandon, "Worship In The Black Experience," in *The Black Christian Worship Experience*, ed. Melva Wilson Costen and Darius Leander Swann (Atlanta: ITC Press, 1992), 114-115.
4. Gayraud S. Wilmore, *Black Religion and Black Radicalism* (Maryknoll: Orbis Books, 1983), 7.
5. Costen, 36-38.
6. Ibid., 15.
7. Albert J. Raboteau, *Slave Religion: The "Invisible Institution" in the Antebellum South* (Oxford: University Press, 1978), 213.
8. Ibid., 213.
9. Brandon, 112-113.
10. John S. Mbiti, *Introduction to African Religion* (Halley Court: Heinemann International Literature and Textbooks, 1991), 60.
11. William Nicholls, *Jacob's Ladder: The Meaning of Worship* (Richmond: Knox Press, 1958), 14.
12. Brandon, 114.
13. Raboteau, 213.
14. Ibid., 213.
15. Edward P. Wimberly, "The Dynamics of Black Worship:

A Psychosocial Exploration of the Impulses That Lie at the Roots of Black Worship," in *The Black Christian Worship Experience*, ed. Melva Wilson Costen and Darius Leander Swann (Atlanta: ITC Press, 1992), 196.

16. Ibid., 198.
17. Mbiti, 62.
18. Harold A. Carter, *The Prayer Tradition of Black People* (Baltimore: Gateway Press, 1990), 23.
19. Ibid., 23.
20. Mbiti, 61.
21. Ibid., 61.
22. Carter, 24.
23. Walker, 28.
24. Carter, 24.
25. Ibid., 31-32.
26. Costen, 106.
27. Ibid., 108.
28. Carter, 89.
29. Costen, 104.
30. Walker, 12.
31. Henry Mitchell, *Black Preaching* (Philadelphia: J. B. Lippincott Company, 1970), 65.
32. Olin P. Moyd, *The Sacred Art: Preaching and Theology in the African American Tradition* (Valley Forge: Judson Press, 1995), 88.
33. J. Alfred Smith, *Preach On!* (Nashville: Broadman Press, 1994), 15.
34. Ibid., 96.
35. Ibid., 96.
36. Ibid., 96.
37. Moyd, 90.
38. Albert J. Raboteau, *A Fire in the Bones* (Boston: Beacon Press, 1995), 142.
39. Moyd, 91.
40. Ibid., 147.
41. Ibid., 144.
42. Ibid., 144.

43. Ibid., 145.
44. Mitchell, 164.
45. Ibid., 164.
46. Ibid., 164.
47. Ibid., 163.
48. Evans E. Crawford, *The Hum* (Nashville: Abingdon Press, 1995), 26-27.
49. Ibid., 173.
50. W. E. B. DuBois, *The Souls of Black Folk* (New York: Library of America, 1903), 138.
51. J. Wendell Mapson, Jr., *The Ministry of Music in the Black Church* (Valley Forge: Judson Press, 1984), 16-18.
52. Walker, 46
53. Mapson, 39.
54. Portia Maultsby, "The Use and Performance of Hymnody, Spirituals, and Gospels in the Black Church," in *The Black Christian Worship Experience*, ed. Melva Wilson Costen and Darius Leander Swann (Atlanta: ITC Press, 1992), 141.
55. Wyatt Tee Walker, *Somebody's Calling My Name* (Valley Forge: Judson Press, 1979), 43.
56. James H. Cone, *The Spirituals and the Blues* (New York: Orbis Books, 1991), 15.
57. Mapson, 36.
58. Cone, 13.
59. Eloise Crosby Culver, *Great American Negroes in Verse* (Washington: The Associated Publishers, Inc., 1966), 19-20.
60. Cone, 13.
61. Maultsby, 153.
62. Ibid., 148.
63. Ibid., 155.
64. Cone, 17.
65. Costen, 99.
66. Ibid., 99
67. Walker, 64.
68. Walker, 75.

69. William B. McClain, *Songs of Zion* (Nashville: Abingdon Press, 1981), 1.
70. Ibid., 1 2.
71. Costen, 98.
72. Walker, 127.
73. Maultsby, 155.
74. Costen, 102.
75. Walker, 128.
76. Wimberly, 195.
77. DuBois, 138-139.

Chapter 4

1. Melva Wilson Costen, *African American Christian Worship* (Nashville: Abingdon Press, 1993), 58.
2. Ibid., 58.
3. Social Science Institute, *God Struck Me Dead: Religious Conversion Experiences and Autobiographies of Negro Ex-Slaves* (Nashville: Fisk University, 1945), v.
4. Ibid.
5. Albert J. Raboteau, *A Fire in the Bones* (Boston: Beacon Press, 1995), 152.
6. Ibid., 153-154.
7. Ibid., 155-156.
8. Ibid., 157.
9. Albert B. Cleage, Jr., *Black Christian Nationalism: New Directions for the Black Church* (Detroit: Luxor Publishers of the Pan-African Orthodox Christian Church, 1972), 74-75.
10. Franklin M. Segler, *Christian Worship: Its Theology and Practice* (Nashville: Broadman Press, 1967), 9.
11. Ibid., 138.
12. Ibid.
13. Ibid., 139
14. Costen, 112.
15. Ibid., 62.
16. Ibid., 63.

17. Ibid., 64.
18. Ibid., 65.
19. Ibid.

Chapter 5

1. Edward T. Hiscox, *The Hiscox Guide for Baptist Churches* (Valley Forge: Judson Press, 1964), 97.
2. James Cone, *My Soul Looks Back* (Nashville: Abingdon Press, 1982), 15.
3. Ibid.
4. Melva Wilson Costen, *African American Christian Worship* (Nashville: Abingdon Press, 1993), 137.
5. Franklin M. Segler, *Christian Worship: Its Theology and Practice* (Nashville: Broadman Press, 1967), 122.
6. Dearing E. King, "Worship in the Black Church," in *Black Church Life-Styles*, comp. Emmanuel L. McCall (Nashville: Broadman Press, 1986), 75.
7. Segler, 129-130.
8. Ibid., 11.

SELECTED BIBLIOGRAPHY

Ammerman, Nancy Tatam *Baptists Battles: Social Change and Religious Conflict in the Southern Baptist Convention* (New Brunswick: Rutgers University Press, 1950), 22.

Aran, Kenneth. et al. *The History of Black Americans.* New York: United Federation of Teachers, 1972.

Bennett, Lerone Jr. *Before the Mayflower: A History of the Negro in America*, 1619-1964, rev. ed. Baltimore: Penguin Books, 1966.

Brackney, William Henry. *The Baptists.* New York: Greenwood Press, 1988.

Brandon, John E. "Worship in the Black Experience." in *The Black Christian Worship Experience*, ed. Melva Wilson Costen and Darius Leander Swann, 109-16. Atlanta: ITC Press, 1992.

Carter, Harold A., Wyatt Tee Walker, and William A. Jones Jr. *The African American Church.* New York: Martin Luther King Fellows Press, 1991.

Carter, Harold A. *The Prayer Tradition of Black People.* Baltimore: Gateway Press, 1990.

Cleage, Albert B. Jr. *Black Christian Nationalism: New Directions for the Black Church.* Detroit: Luxor Publishers of the Pan-African Orthodox Christian Church, 1972.

Cone, James H. *God of the Oppressed.* New York: Seabury Press, 1975.

The Spirituals and the Blues. Valley Forge: Judson Press, 1979.

My Soul Looks Back. Nashville: Abingdon Press, 1982.

103

Costen, Melva Wilson. *African American Christian Worship.* Nashville: Abingdon Press, 1993.

Crawford, Evans E. *The Hum.* Nashville: Abingdon Press, 1995.

Culver, Eloise Crosby. *Great American Negroes in Verse.* Washington, D.C.: The Associated Publishers, Inc., 1966.

DuBois, W. E. B. *The Souls of Black Folk.* Chicago: McClurg, 1903; repr., New York: New American Library, 1969.

Evans, James H. Jr. *We Have Been Believers: An African-American Systematic Theology.* Minneapolis: Fortress Press, 1992.

Franklin, John Hope. "George Washington Williams and Africa in *Africa and the Afro-American Experience,* ed. Lorraine A. williams, 59-76. Washington, D.C.: Howard University Press, 1977.

Franklin, John Hope and Alfred A. Moss Jr. *From Slavery to Freedom: A History of Negro Americans.* New York: Alfred A. Knopf Inc., 1947.

Fitts, Leroy. A *History of Black Baptists.* Nashville: Broadman Press, 1985.

Hiscox, Edward T. *The Hiscox Guide for Baptist Churches.* Valley Forge: Judson Press, 1964.

Hoyt, Thomas Jr. "The African American Worship Experience and The Bible." *The Journal of the Interdenominational Theological Center.* ed. Melva Wilson Costen and Darius Leander Swann, 1-22. Atlanta: ITC Press, 1992.

King, Dearing E. "Worship in the Black Church." *Black Church Life-Styles.* comp. Emmanuel L. McCall. Nashville: Broadman Press, 1986.

Lefler, Hugh T. Winston-Salem. *World Book Encyclopedia*. 1974 ed.

Mapson, J. Wendell Jr. *The Ministry of Music in the Black Church*. Valley Forge: Judson Press, 1984.

Maultsby, Portia. "The Use and Performance of Hymnody, Spirituals, and Gospels in the Black Church" in *The Black Christian Worship Experience*. ed. Melva Wilson Costen and Darius Leander Swann, 141-60. Atlanta: ITC Press, 1992.

Mbiti, John S. *Introduction to African Religion*. Halley Court: Heinemann International Literature and Textbooks, 1991.

African Religions and Philosophy. Garden City, NY: Anchor Books, 1970.

McClain, William B. *Songs of Zion*. Nashville: Abingdon Press, 1981.

McCullough, Yvette. *Blacks Find Keys to Unlock Racial Barriers*. Winston-Salem Chronicle. 17 March 1979.

Mitchell, Henry. *Black Preaching*. Philadelphia: J.B. Lippincott Co., 1970.

Moyd, Olin P. *The Sacred Art: Preaching and Theology in the African American Tradition*. Valley Forge: Judson Press, 1995.

Nicholls, William. *Jacob's Ladder: The Meaning of Worship*. Richmond: Knox Press, 1958.

1960-70: "The Civil Rights Movement." Winston-Salem Chronicle. 24 March 1979.

Pitts, Walter F. *Old Ship of Zion: The Afro-Baptist Ritual in the African Diaspora*. New York: Oxford University Press, 1993.

Pollard, Alton B. III. "Race, Religion, and Resistance in The African American Experience." Speech delivered at the Associacao Nacional Casa Dandara International Seminar, Minas-Centro/Belo Horizonte, Minas Gerais Brazil, 5-10 November 1995.

Quarles, Benjamin. *The Negro in the Making of America.* London: Collier-Macmillan LTD, 1964.

Raboteau, Albert J. *Slave Religion: The "Invisible Institution" in the Antebellum South.* Oxford: University Press, 1978.

A Fire in the Bones. Boston: Beacon Press, 1995.

Segler, Franklin M. *Christian Worship: Its Theology and Practice.* Nashville: Broadman Press, 1967.

John E. Skoglund, *The Baptists* (Valley Forge: Judson Press, 1967), 10-12.

Smith, J. Alfred. *Preach On!* Nashville: Broadman Press, 1994.

Sobel, Mechal. *Trablin' On: The Slave Journey to an Afro-Baptist Faith.* Westport: Greenwood Press, 1969.

Social Science Institute. *God Struck Me Dead: Religious Conversion Experiences and Autobiographies of Negro Ex-Slaves.* Nashville: Fisk University, 1945.

Tursi, Frank V. *Winston-Salem: A History.* Winston-Salem: John F. Blair Publisher, 1994.

Walker, Wyatt Tee. *The Soul of Black Worship.* New York: Martin Luther King Fellows Press, 1984.

Somebody's Calling My Name. Valley Forge: Judson Press, 1979.

Washington, James Melvin. *Frustrated Fellowship: The Black Baptist Quest for Social Power.* Macon: Mercer University Press, 1963.

Weatherford, W. D. *American Churches and the Negro: An Historical Study from Early Slave Days to the Present.* Boston: Christopher Publishing House, 1957.

Wilmore, Gayraud S. *Black Religion and Black Radicalism: An Interpretation of the Religious History of Afro-American People.* Maryknoll: Orbis Books, 1983.

Wimberly, Edward P. "The Dynamics of Black Worship: A Psychosocial Exploration of the Impulses That Lie at the Roots of Black Worship." in *The Black Christian Worship Experience.* Atlanta: ITC Press, 1992.

GLOSSARY

The definitions of the words contained in this glossary are supplied by the author with the intention of providing meaning to the materials provided in this book.

A Cappella: Singing without instrumental accompaniment.

African-American Baptist church: An American black cultured denomination within the mainstream of the United States, in that, it has evolved out of the Baptist tradition of Protestantism and the government of which is in the hands of African Americans.

African-American culture sermons: Sermons focusing on the social behavior patterns and beliefs of Americans.

African-American worship: The visible acting out of what African Americans believe about God based on their history; how they see and respond to God.

African-American slave trade: The business of buying, transporting, and selling African-American slaves.

Antislavery movement: A group of people working together to bring about the end of slavery.

Associations: Organizations confined to a certain area within a state.

Baptism: Baptism for Baptists is defined as immersion in water of a believer in Christ symbolizing the faith of the believer in a crucified, buried, and risen Savior.

Baptist: One who believes in the Baptist distinctives of the Christian religion.

Benediction: The benediction is given to commend the worshipers to God's care and announce His blessings upon them.

Call-and-response: A dialogue between the preacher and the congregation.

Chanting: The intentional timing in the use of words, phrases, and sentences and delivered in rhythmic, metrical speech.

Conversion: The change from unbelief to faith that represent a change of heart, a transformation in consciousness, and a reorientation of personality.

Dehumanize: To deprive a person of human qualities and freedoms.

Distinguish: To recognize the qualities and features of a thing that give it its special character and set it apart from others.

Emancipation: Being set free from slavery.

Environment: The surrounding conditions and influences that affect the development of a living thing.

Folk ways: The way of thinking and acting adopted by African Americans as part of their shared culture.

Great awakenings: Revival services.

Improvise: To sing a song different from the way it is written by making slight variations to words, tune, and/or timing.

Lord's Supper: Jesus' last supper with His disciples before His crucifixion. The bread and wine served at the supper symbolized His body and blood, respectively, and His sacrifice for humanity.

Mannerisms: The way (preachers) freely express themselves with behaviors unrelated to the message.

Meter: The arrangement of beats in music describing a newly shaped folk-form originating with hymns by Isaac Watts.

Mourners' bench: Usually the front pew in the church where those who were not Christians but had the desire to become Christians would sit during revival services in anticipation of receiving salvation.

Musical repertoire: The accumulated supply of songs prepared to perform.

Oppression: To be forced to live in a manner that is unjust and cruel.

Oppressors: People who are cruel or unjust to people under them.

Preaching style: The way in which a preacher uses language and feelings in expressing thought.

Racism: Involves a form of subjection of one race by another.

Reconstruction: The political process by which the defeated Southern States, which had seceded from the Union, again became part of the United States.

Share-croppers: People who farm land for the owner in return for part of the crops.

Segregation: The separation of a race from other races in schools, restaurants, theaters, neighborhoods, etc.

Slavery: The custom of owning slaves.

Social history: A statement of past events dealing with the living conditions and treatment of a group of people.

Socialization: The act of being concerned with human beings in their relations to each other.

Spontaneity: Something that is not forced but caused by natural impulse or desire.

Thicket: A cluster of small trees growing close together.

Tradition: The handing down of beliefs, opinions, customs, stories, etc., from parents to children or from one generation to the other.

Whooping: A sing-song style of preaching.

Worship: The act of according God with due recognition, praise, and honor.

NAME INDEX

Breinigsville, PA USA
29 June 2010
240802BV00002B/1/A